Oregon State Prison
Superintendents
The Shepherds of State Street
1864-2009
by
Sue Woodford-Beals and
Carl E. Beals

Visitors first view of lobby inside Oregon State Penitentiary - Grill work created by inmates in ironwork program
OSP Photo

Copyright © 2009 Sue Woodford-Beals and Carl E. Beals
All rights reserved. No part of this book may be reproduced or transmitted in any form or by any means, electronic or mechanical, including photocopying, recording or by any information storage and retrieval system, without written permission from the publisher, except for the inclusion of brief quotations in a review. Mail inquiries to Airy Woods Publishing Company, P.O. Box 3692, Salem, Or 97302

Oregon State Prison
The Shepherds of State Street
1864-2009
by Sue Woodford-Beals and Carl E. Beals

Includes index
ISBN 978-0-578-03564-2
First Edition 2009

Airy Woods Publishing Company
P.O. Box 3692
Salem, OR 97302

Printed and bound in the USA using paper made in the USA

Note on photo reverse side: About 1900 tours of the prison were conducted by staff. Visitors were given the opportunity to made a donation in a box in the lobby to provide literature for inmates. Some prisons charged an admission fee. OSP did not charge a fee for tours.

This book is dedicated to the men and women of the Oregon State Corrections Association of Retirees (OSCAR) whose encouragement and assistance have made it possible

Early Stage and Theater in the OSP dining room. The theater was used for live performances as well as for showing films. An inmate clerk is seated on the stage.

Inmate Band 1960s

Table of Contents

In The Beginning 1
Alva Compton Riggs Shaw 7
Major Montgomery P. Berry. 11
William H. Watkinds 15
Benjamin Franklin Burch 19
Asahel Bush 21
Julius Augustus Stratton 23
George Collins 25
George S. Downing 28
Andrew Nathan Gilbert 31
Joseph Daniel Lee: 34
Charles W. James 41
Frank Hamilton Curtis 46
Berton K. Lawson 47
Harry Percy Minto 49
John W. Minto 51
Charles A. Murphy 54
Robert L. Stevens 57
Robert E. Lee Steiner, MD 59
Louis Hartt Compton 62
James W. Lewis 65
Johnson S. Smith 66
Amos M. Dalrymple 68
John William "Will" Lillie 71
Henry W. Meyers 73
James W. Lewis 77
George Cassie Alexander 83
Virgil J. O'Malley 85
Clarence Theron Gladden 87
Hoyt Carl Cupp 103
J.C. Verl Keeney 108
Manfred (Fred) Maass 110
Nick Armenakis 112
S. Frank Thompson, Jr. 113
Mitch Morrow 114
Joan Palmateer 115
Stan Czerniak 117
Brian Belleque 118
Authors 121
End Notes 122
Acknowledgments 123

Index 124
Executions in Oregon 129
Executions in Oregon 1851 to 2008 132
Uniforms 136
Uniforms 137
Uniforms 138
Letter from Treasury Department 139
A Tribute to Sergeant Joe Johnson 143
OSP History Told in Law Enforcement Magazine 143
"You Are There" 143
OSP 88 Years Ago 1867 - 1955 143
Boys Training School Cemetery 145
Map of State Prisons 147
Inmate Art Work 148

Early Salem Electric Street Car transporting visitors to the State House, Prison and Asylum

In The Beginning

1851 Legislative Assembly of the Territory of Oregon appointed Hugh O'Bryant, D.H. Lonsdale and Lucius Hastings to a board of commissioners to superintend the erection of a territorial penitentiary.

1852 In the winter of 1852-53, at a session of the assembly, a new commission was appointed consisting of Messrs.: William King, Shubrick Norris and S. Parker to locate and build a territorial penitentiary. Under direction of this commission the original prison was located in Portland, The contract entered into for a building of stone and brick at an estimated cost of $85,000. It was a financial disaster, and was later sold by the commission for $6,000.

1853 During the legislative session of 1853-54 the former commissioners were removed and W.S. Ladd, A.D. Fitch and D.H. Belknap were appointed, who supervised the completion of the territorial penitentiary and selection of Joseph Sloane, February 1854 as Keeper. At the time there were three prisoners but on the day Mr. Sloane took charge, one of these prisoners escaped. They were housed in a one story frame building on Front Street during the time the penitentiary was being constructed.

1855 A new board of commissioners was appointed composed of Joseph Sloane, S.J. McCormick and W.P. Doland. The Territorial Penitentiary in Portland was completed in 1856 and the prisoners were moved to it.

1856 At the legislative session of 1856-57 the board of commissioners was abolished and the management of the prisoners was turned over to a superintendent appointed by the Territorial Governor, George L. Curry. Curry appointed Joseph Sloane who served until June 22, 1859 when that office was abolished. There were 35 prisoners in custody at that time. See letter in Appendices to Governor Curry.

1859 Oregon Statehood on February 14. The management of the penitentiary was contracted out to Robert Newall and Levi English by Governor John Whitaker, the first governor of the State of Oregon.

1862 The legislature abolished the contract and the governor was made ex-officio superintendent of the penitentiary. This not being satisfactory, was changed as soon as possible and in 1864 the legislature again created a policy of having a superintendent appointed by the governor.

1864 Alva Compton Riggs Shaw was appointed the first superintendent of the Oregon State Penitentiary. He supervised about 23 inmates at the Portland prison, before the penitentiary was built in Salem. Salem had been reaffirmed as the city where the capitol was to be located — a disastrous fire had destroyed the capitol and debate ensued before it was decided the state prison would be located in Salem. Shaw was charged with the responsibility of finding an appropriate place to build the prison in Salem.

1865 The purchase of the State Street property along Mill Creek in Salem was announced. The total cost was $9,019.

1866 In May Superintendent Shaw moves 23 prisoners from Portland to a temporary prison in Salem at the State Street property.

1870 The legislature appropriated $50,000 to build a permanent penitentiary.

1871 The Oregon State Penitentiary is completed in Salem.

Before the Oregon State Penitentiary was located in Salem in 1866, a territorial penitentiary was built in Portland on the corner of Front and Harrison Streets.

The Portland building was later sold for $6,000 gold coin. It was discovered at the time of sale that less than one-third of the building was on state land and the remainder was on private property.

The territorial prison in Portland, about 1860. It was built on two blocks, with a street dividing the facility.

The Ill-Fated Portland Prison

Oregon was under provisional government from 1843 to 1849 during this time outlaws were held in small local jails under jurisdiction of the sheriff. Joe Meek was appointed Oregon sheriff. In 1849 a territorial governor was appointed by the president. Joe Meek was appointed as a territorial marshal. The marshal and deputies could arrest and detain outlaws but needed a larger, more secure place to hold them.

A legislative assembly appointed commissioners to supervise the construction of a territorial prison. This prison was located on block 107 and fractional block 106 in Portland. These two blocks were split by a street, dividing the prison property. This division made the land functionally inappropriate for use as a prison.

Another glitch came to light when the state attempted to sell the property, Major Montgomery Berry reported August 31, 1868, "Had the building been located upon land belonging to the state, as it was supposed to be when constructed, it would have brought double the amount obtained — but less than one third of the building was on state land, and the remainder on private property, the price for which it sold was all that could be made out of it."

Running The Prison

Managing the Oregon State Penitentiary in 1864 required a different type of knowledge, skill and ability than the same job requires today. Although the position description has changed over the years and those filling that position changed frequently in one hundred and forty three years, all who served brought one quality to the job; dedication to service. Each person appointed was proud to have been selected and appears to have worked diligently to perform the duties as they viewed them at the time of their appointment. Some appeared to have been more successful in the eyes of the public and the administration than others. Never the less, from historical documents it seems that each superintendent worked hard to fulfill the requirements of the job.

In the early years four of those appointed had law degrees; Asahal Bush, Julius Stratton, George Downing and Robert L. Stevens. One appointee, Benjamin F. Burch was a minister who came to the work from a faith perspective. Robert E. Lee Steiner was the only superintendent who was a physician and a very capable business manager. Three had been employed as teachers; Charles James, Johnson Smith, and J.C. Keeney. Three others had also been employed in the newspaper business; William H. Watkinds, Asahel Bush and Johnson Smith. Two had been printers; Julius Stratton and Amos Dalrymple. Benjamin Burch, Andrew Gilbert, Joseph D. Lee and Johnson Smith had served in the Legislature. Most of those chosen had a strong interest in politics and took an active part in community affairs.

Inmates cleaning buckets used as latrines cell block B as late as 1950s

Success in business appeared to be the primary qualification for; George Collins, Andrew Gilbert, Joseph Lee, Berton K. Lawson, John W. Minto, and Amos Dalrymple. Law enforcement and Corrections experience was a leading qualification for Harry P. Minto, John Minto, John William "Will" Lillie, George C. Alexander, Virgil O'Malley, C.T. Gladden, H. C. Cupp, J.C, Keeney, M. Fred Maass, Frank Thompson, Joan Palmateer, Stan Czerniak and Brian Belleque.

Most of these superintendents demonstrated an awareness of the value of subordinate staff who managed the operations of the prison twenty four hours a day, seven days a week. In 1928 guards, worked seven days a week with no vacation. Most guards, lived on the penitentiary reservation in the officers quarters where they ate and slept.

The superintendents who have served during the past 50 years have had a thorough knowledge of correctional administration and operations, including records maintenance, security practices, and the supervision of inmates.

Most of these superintendents possessed outstanding communication and organization skills. By necessity they acclimate to the whims of the legislature so are flexible and able to adapt to ever changing unfunded mandates. They acquire knowledge of policies, procedures, laws, and regulations governing the operation of a complex prison operation. All this in addition to understanding the need to exhibit the leadership qualities that engender the confidence of both the staff and the public.

With the ever increasing instances of litigation by inmates over every aspect of the environment in which they live from the food they are served to the towels issued for showers, the stamina to withstand this barrage of law suits is critical. In the early days of the Oregon State Penitentiary the superintendents would not have dreamed that they would be sued over mail not delivered or the amount of legal documents an inmate is allowed in a cell. These issues were moot in 1864 and in 1924. As late as 1954 some cell blocks at Oregon State Penitentiary still had only cold running water and buckets for latrines. Superintendents today are faced with continuing maintenance problems with this one hundred and forty three year old structure. Many improvements have been made to the physical plant but each new addition has added another layer of wiring, plumbing, and security issues.

Today there are more than thirteen correctional institutions. Some allow inmates to posses television sets as well as video games in their cells.

Gladiator Newsletter Volume 5, Number 3, Wednesday, March 25, 1959
1870 Prison Rule book Found

In the late 1930s a brick structure served as the administration building of the Oregon State Penitentiary and was located on the same site as the present administration building. when this old building was removed to make way for the present one, a lead box was removed from the cornerstone of the older building. The box contained numerous mementos, curious and interesting, of the era when the penitentiary was first located in Salem. Among these articles was a rule book, titled "Rules and Regulations for the government of the penitentiary, 1870." The following rules transcribed here were taken from that rule book...

Rule 5: "The Warden shall take care that all rules of the government of the guards and of the prison and for the discipline of the prisoners are properly enforced. He shall see that the prison is kept clean and that all parts are in good order and condition throughout the building; that the prisoners are clean in person and clothing; that they are properly secured when in or about the prison; that their chains and shackles are in proper order when they are given in charge of the Assistant Warden or guards. He shall personally inspect the shackles of every prisoner when lined up in the morning for duty and shall count the prisoners in the line before turning them over to the Assistant Warden who shall in turn count them and call back the number to the Warden. He shall at the same time and place enter the number in a book to be kept for that purpose and also issue to the prisoners their daily rations of tobacco."

Rule 7: "Officers and employees will be required to observe strictly the following regulations; That no tale bearing to and fro between the prison and the city concerning brother officers will be allowed. Any officer so offending will be dismissed provided that it shall be the duty of each officer to report to the superintendent any violation of rules or neglect of duty."

Rule 13: "No officer or guard shall use harsh or immoral language to any convict or to one another, nor shall they jest with any convict."

Assistant Editor, SGT Joe Johnson

Timeline

1851 Legislative Assembly of the Territory of Oregon appointed Hugh O'Bryant, D.H. Lonsdale and Lucius Hastings to a board of commissioners to superintend the erection of a territorial penitentiary.

From 1862 to 1913 the Penitentiary Superintendent was appointed by the Governor, in 1913 appointment was by the Board of Control. By 1917 appointment was back under the Governor, later repealed in 1927 and returned to the Board of Control, resulting in frequent changes in management, in response to political influence. In 1953 appointment came under the jurisdiction of the state civil service commission.

1928 The State Training School for Boys buildings deeded to the Oregon State Penitentiary as a Farm Annex
1949 South Fork Forest Camp established
1959 Oregon State Correctional Institution built
1964 The Oregon Womens Corrections Center built
1965 The Board of Control appoints the first Director of Corrections
1968 Riot occurs
1968 Marion County Grand Jury recommends director be fired

1977 Prigg Cottage retrofitted opened as release center
1977 Women Release Unit opens at State Hospital
1985 The Eastern Oregon Correction Institution retrofitted opened as a prison in Pendleton
1989 Powder River Correctional Facility opened in Baker City
1990 Shutter Creek Correctional Facility opens in North Bend
1990 Columbia River Correctional Institution opens in Portland
1991 Snake River Correctional Institution opens in Ontario
2000 Two Rivers Correctional Institution opens in Hermiston
2001 Coffee Creek Correctional Facility opens in Wilsonville
2002 Oregon Womens Correctional Center returned to OSP
2005 Warner Creek Correctional Facility opens in Lakeview
2007 Deer Ridge Correctional Facility opens in Madras

Superintendents of Oregon State Penitentiary 1864 to 2009

1. Alva Compton Riggs Shaw . . . . October 24,1864 to September 13, 1866
2. Major Montgomery P. Berry . . . . . . September 14, 1866 - September 14, 1870
3. William H. Watkinds . . . . September 14, 1870 - February 14,1877
4. Benjamin Franklin Burch. . . . . February 18. 1877 - October 31, 1878
5. Asahel Bush. . . . . October 31, 1878 - December 4, 1882
6. Judge Julius A. Stratton . . . . December 4, 1882 - October 14, 1884
7. George Collins. . . . . October 14, 1884 - February 1, 1887
8. George S. Downing . . . . March 13, 1888 - March 9, 1895
9. Andrew Nathan Gilbert . . . . March 11, 1895 - 1899
10. Joseph D. Lee. . . . . April 1, 1899 - April 1, 1903
11. Charles W. James. . . . . April 1,1903 - May 6, 1912
12. Frank H. Curtis. . . . . May 7, 1912 - September 30, 1912
13. Berton K. Lawson . . . . October 1, 1912 - March 8, 1915
14. Harry Percy Minto . . . . March 23, 1915 - September 27, 1915
15. John W. Minto . . . . September 28, 1915 - November 27, 1916
16. Captain Charles A. Murphy . . . . . . November 27, 1916 - December 3, 1918
17. Robert L. Stevens. . . . . December 3, 1918 - May 30, 1919
18. Dr. Robert E. Lee Steiner . . . . May 30, 1919 - February 1, 1920
19. Louis H. Compton . . . . February 1, 1920 - May 1, 1922
20. James W. Lewis . . . . May 1, 1922 - January 15, 1923
21. Johnson S. Smith . . . . January 15, 1923 - October 8, 1923
22. Amos M. Dalrymple . . . . October 8, 1923 - December 5, 1925
23. John William Lillie . . . . December 5, 1925 - April 1, 1927
24. Henry W. Meyers. . . . . April 1, 1927 - May 1, 1931
25. James W. Lewis . . . . October 1, 1931 - October 28, 1938
26. George C. Alexander . . . . December 15, 1938 - April 1953
27. Virgil J. O'Malley . . . . September 1951 - April 1953
28. Clarence T. Gladden . . . . April 1953 - March 1968
29. Hoyt Carl Cupp . . . . March 9, 1968 - August 31, 1984
30. J. C. Keeney . . . . September 1, 1984 - July 31, 1986
31. Manfred (Fred) Maass . . . . August 1, 1986 - June 1994
32. Frank Thompson . . . . December 1, 1994 - April, 1998
33. Joan Palmateer. . . . . April 1, 1998 - February 2001
34. Stan Czerniak. . . . . February 1, 2001
35. Brian Belleque . . . . June 2003

* The dates of appointment and resignation of the first nine superintendents are contained in the 1895 biennial report.

Alva Compton Riggs Shaw
October 29, 1864 -
September 14, 1866.

A. C. R. Shaw was born in 1816 in New York state He was a pioneer sheep rancher and real estate promoter. He and his foster-father, Joshua Shaw, drove a band of sheep from Illinois to Oregon in 1844. He became co-founder of Cincinnati, Oregon (later named, Eola). He was married January 22, 1846 to Sarah Eleanor McNary in Polk County. He and Sarah were the parents of five children; Lucien, Eunice, Olive, Mary, and Holt.

Shaw was the first superintendent serving in Salem. He was responsible for locating property developing it and moving inmates from Portland to the first temporary structure in Salem. In March 1865 a site for the prison was selected along Mill Creek. [1]

May 16, 1866, twenty three inmates were moved from Portland to Salem. During this time the Gardner Shackle was put into use because of the number of escapes.

Photo OSP

The legislature commissioned Shaw, J. H. Moores and Reverend George Atkinson to secure land and erect the penitentiary. Atkinson visited several western prisons and studied the construction, management and employment.[2] The layout plan of OSP was based upon Atkinson's detailed report.[2]

Shaw was required to clear the land, build the fence and begin construction of a brick prison building. He purchased the land for the prison at $45.00 per acre which included 147 acres of the land where the Oregon State Hospital is located ($6,615) and the water rights ($2,000) for a total of $8,615. He was responsible for making all the purchases for the prison and he exercised great care and economy in that process. Food costs were reported to be twenty three and one half cents per day per inmate.

The first temporary wood structure consisted of lodging for the convicts, a cook house, and dining shed, together with an office for the superintendent. Brick making was started and two hundred and fifty thousand brick were fired in preparation for constructing the permanent prison building. The clay was obtained from the adjoining land owned by Morgan L. Savage and was transported to the prison by a temporary railway.

On August 17, 1866, superintendent Shaw, warden Seth Allard and brickyard foreman Alden were seized by a large group of convicts armed with butcher knives in an attempt to escape. Shaw, Allard and Alden were saved when guards opened fire upon the convicts. This incident described in detail in the Statesman newspaper, September 3, 1866, undoubtedly contributed to Shaw's interest in leaving the position of superintendent.

Charley Clatawed had the distinction of being prisoner number one and he received a three year sentence for stealing horses.

In an article describing the brick making and construction process the Oregon Statesman newspaper of August 20, 1866, announced Shaw's resignation.[3]

Oral history reveals that after Shaw sold his donation land claim in Polk County, he traveled to Santa Rosa, California, where he is said to have farmed. He later relocated to Berkeley. The Shaw family is in the 1880 U.S. Census living in Berkeley, records list Alva, his wife, Sarah McNary, and their four children. He died August 8, 1880 in Berkeley.

His daughter in law Mrs. Holt R. (Loma Scroggins) Shaw donated a collection of early Oregon newspapers along with letters written by A. C. R. Shaw from the Oregon country in 1845 and 1848 to the Oregon Historical Society. An oddity in the collection is a piece of blanket woven from the wool of the first sheep driven in 1844 over what was to become the old Oregon trail.

Two of the more interesting inmates received during Shaw's tenure were: Charity Lamb and Indian Charley Clatawed. Charley Clatawed had the distinction of being prisoner number one and he received a three year sentence for stealing horses. He was received around July 1853, he escaped December 3, 1853, he was recaptured May 5, 1859 and escaped June 16, 1862.

Number of employees: 16
Number of inmates: 211 inmates were received between July 16, 1853 and August 31, 1866.
Number of escapes: 115 escapes had occurred by September 1866.
Recaptured: 58 inmates
At large: 67 inmates [4]

In Polk County, Mr. Shaw's' land claim was located on highway 22, now named the Brunk House. It is in this house that the Shaws lived prior to their move to California.
Photo Sue Woodford

The Oregon boot

The boot was placed on one leg only. This kept the inmate off balance and deprived him of agility.

At the time the Oregon Boot was invented, the territorial prison and later the penitentiary had an enormous escape problem. J. C. Gardner and subsequent wardens and guards felt that the inmate population could not be adequately controlled without using the Gardner Shackle on each and every prisoner.

When Gardner was replaced as a warden, he obtained a court order preventing the use of the shackle without payment to him. The Oregon legislature did authorize the payment of funds to Gardner that same year.

Wearing the shackle for extended periods of time caused extreme physical damage. Inmates would be bedridden for weeks at a time in extreme pain. The Gardner Shackles became known as man-killers to the prisoners who wore them.

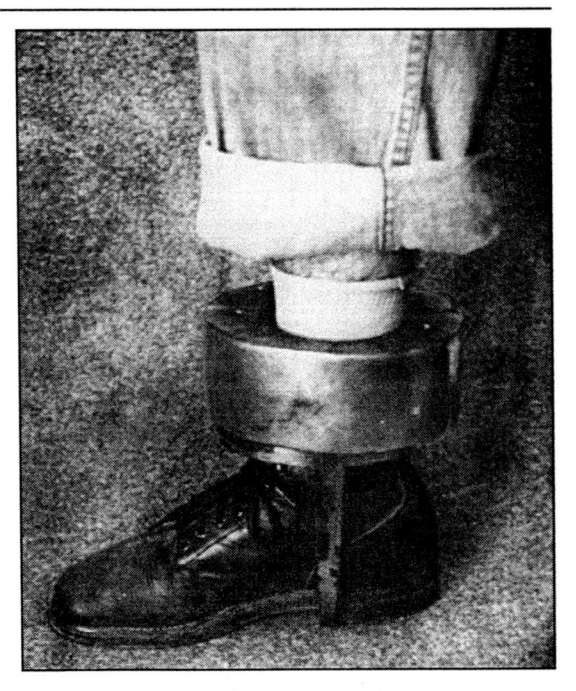

The Oregon Boot AKA: Gardner Shackle

The Oregon Department of Corrections reports, "The Oregon Boot," or Gardner Shackle as it was properly known, was patented July 3, 1866 by, then Oregon State Penitentiary warden, J. C. Gardner. The shackles were manufactured at the penitentiary by prisoners. Each shackle consisted of a heavy iron band that locked around one ankle. This iron band was supported by another iron ring and braces which attached to the heel of a boot. These shackles weighed between 5 and 28 pounds a piece.

Superintendent Burch in a report to the Governor in 1878 stated:" Such punishment can never lead to reformation hence I determined to dispense with the shackle except as punishment."

During Watkinds administration the prison physician James A. Richardson made the following recommendation to the superintendent for inclusion in his report to Governor L. F. Grover:

"Kidney and spinal troubles have been quite common, induced in many cases, I think, by wearing the Gardner shackle. The continued application of this great weight of from 6 to 28 pounds to the lower extremities must of necessity destroy the muscular power of the lower limbs. But, what I deem the most serious evil is this: With from 6 to 28 pounds of cold iron around the ankles the prisoners must of necessity, with the ordinary supply of bedding furnished to prisoners, suffer with cold feet and limbs during the nights, which in this climate are always cool. And the effect of continually cold extremities cannot result otherwise than disastrously to the health of the convict. I would, therefore, in the strongest terms, recommend that means be adopted at the earliest possible moment to dispense altogether with the Gardner Shackle".

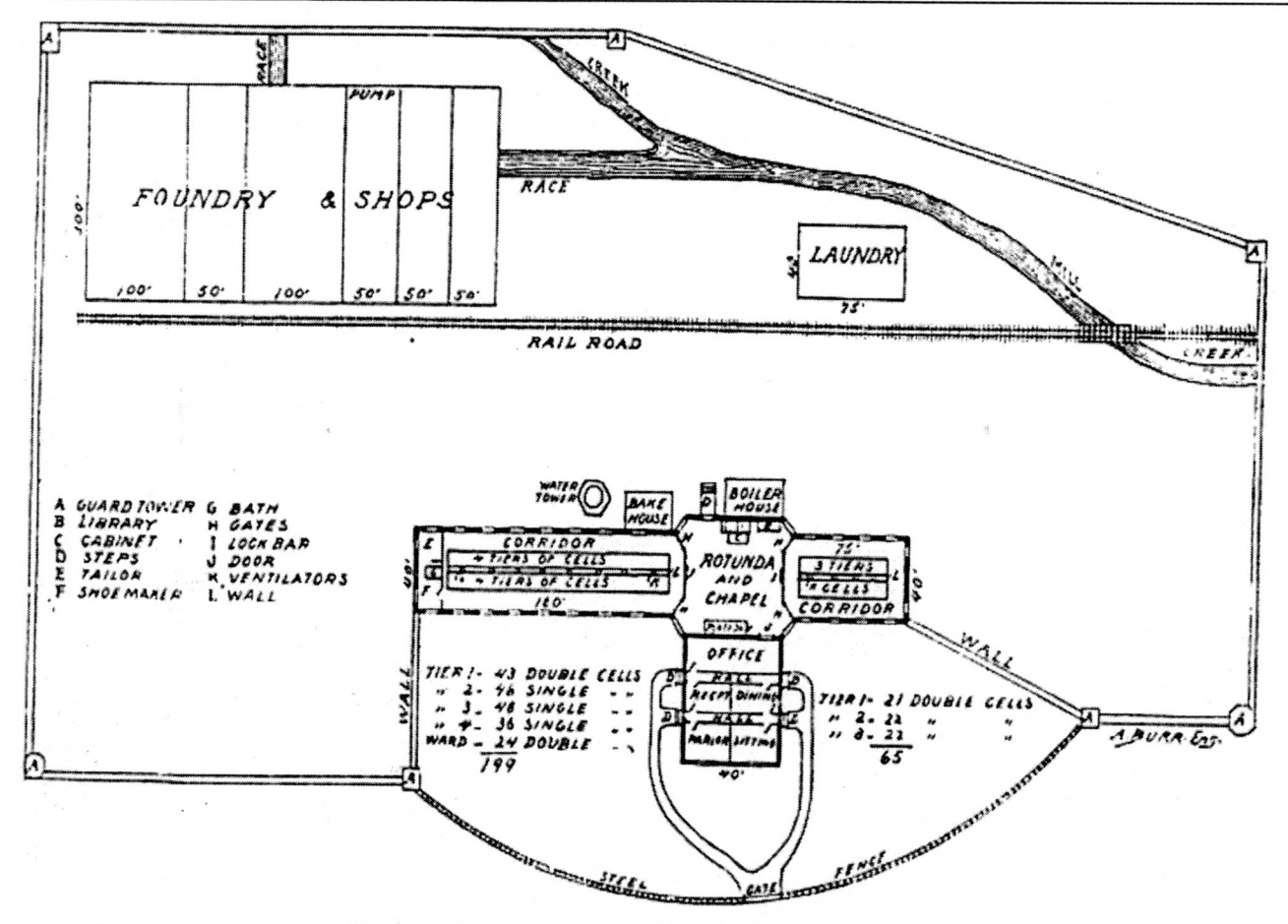

GENERAL PLAN OF THE OREGON STATE PENITENTIARY.

The first female prisoner on record was sentenced for murdering her husband. She was Charity Lamb. She plunged an ax into her husbands head and was convicted of murder in the second degree. The Oregonian Newspaper of September 30, 1854 further stated that she said, "I didn't mean to kill the critter, I only intended to stun him."[5]

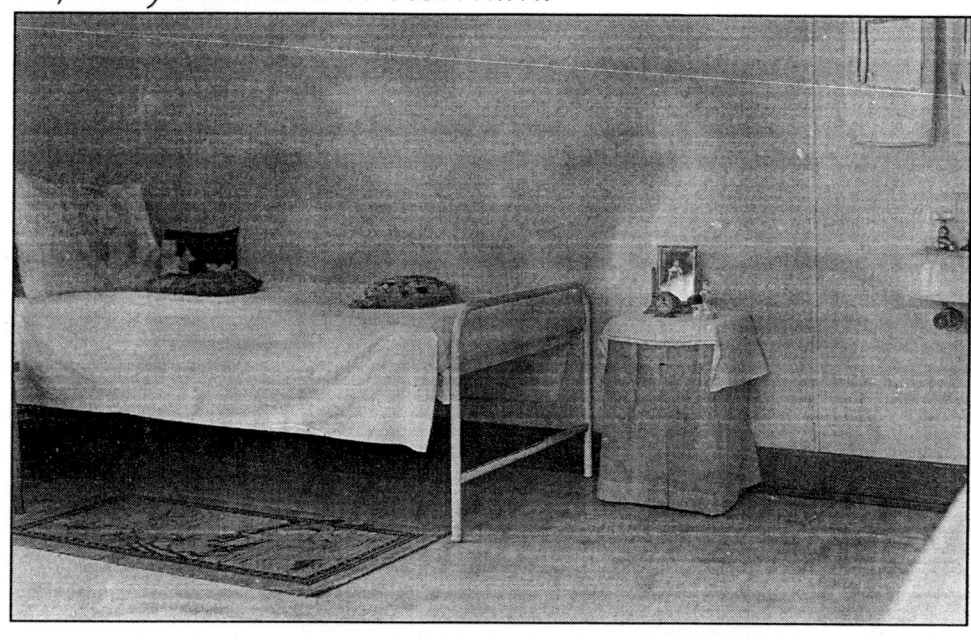

A cell in the women's ward at OSP located in the Administration Building until Oregon Women's Correctional Center was built in 1965

Major Montgomery P. Berry
September 14, 1866 – September 14, 1870

Photo courtesy Kathy Milne

Major Montgomery Pike Berry was born in 1827 in Kentucky. He was in the military and traveled in that capacity, serving in the Mexican War. He lived in Fort Leavenworth, Kansas territory, in 1857 and with his wife is found in the 1860 census in Atchison, Kansas territory He gained the rank of Major from having raised three companies of federal troops during the civil campaign. He and his wife Sara Isabella moved to Oregon in 1861 and lived in Wasco county When Wasco county was created on January 11, 1854, it consisted of all of Oregon Territory between the Cascade Range and the Rocky Mountains and from the California border to the Washington border. This was the largest county ever formed in the United States. Major Berry was a good friend of George L. Woods, Wasco county judge at the time Grant county was formed from Wasco county. Berry was elected the first sheriff of Grant county and served in that position from 1862 to 1866. On August 3, 1865 sheriff Berry presided over the hanging of William Kane sentenced to death for first degree murder. Kane's skull is on display in the Grant County Museum in Canyon City identified as the second man hung in Grant County.

Berry was appointed as Superintendent of Oregon State Penitentiary on September 14, 1866 by George L. Woods two days after Woods was elected governor. Berry and his wife Sarah Isabella Berry settled into the Salem community taking part in various community activities. Sarah was a friend of Louisa Woods, wife of the governor and the two women took music lessons together at Sacred Heart Academy.

Taking over the management of the prison was a daunting job for Berry. His predecessor, Shaw was commended for establishment of the prison and moving the convicts to Salem but was criticized for not preventing many escapes. It was thought that the new facility lacked discipline. Berry was appointed to instill military efficiency and discipline in the prison. He brought with him W. B. Morse of Yamhill county and J. M. Gale, a former lieutenant in the Oregon Infantry.

Regarding the operation of the prison, the Salem American Unionist reports, "Major Berry has effected a wonderful reformation in the workings of the establishment, and is in a fair way to relieve this commonwealth of excessive burden by the skillful and successful application of the prison's productive resources."[6]

In Berry's report to the governor September 1, 1868 he says, "At the time of entering upon the duty assigned to me, it was a totally new field of labor, and one which I had never contemplated, excepting, as other citizens from a distance; and when brought into immediate contact therewith, realized that fine spun theories upon the control of convicts and the utilizing of their labor sufficiently to make them pay the annual expenditures made on their behalf, was one branch of the subject, and the actual proceeding was another."[7]

His concern for untrained staff working as guards in this new prison caused him to comment, "The continual strain upon their vigilance either wears them out, so much that they retire voluntarily, or they become careless and have to be removed." He introduced a supernumerary system where officers were placed on half salaries while they learned the business, their promotion assured upon a vacancy occurring in the regular line.

Berry's changes included increasing the night patrol, using vacant cells in the lower tier as hospital beds as no hospital area was built in the original plans. He provided an area where school was taught by better educated fellow inmates.

He lamented that many men discharged from prison had no clothes to wear out due to the wilful neglect by staff of caring for inmate property. He furnished clothing for them. Regarding underclothing for prisoners he stated; underclothing is unknown in this prison, unless ordered by the physician for isolated cases. In nearly all other prisons from which reports have been received regular returns of underclothing are made. He proposed that some good strong cloth be introduced for underclothing.

He recommended changes in the use of inmates as kitchen help for officers mess. He thought it endangered the officers. He wanted a building constructed for living quarters for officers with a mess house erected therein where they would cook their own food.

His recommendations on discipline are as follows:
Punishment for violation of institution rules:
First offense: Lecture from supervisory officer
Second offense: Reported to superintendent to admonish the culprit.
Third offense: Carries a shackle, if he already has one a second one is placed on the first one.
Fourth offense: Reported to the superintendent who in most cases gives offender a sanction of bread and water from 1 to 10 days in solitary.
Flogging was used as a last resort and then only when the prisoner breached every rule of discipline or committed an outrage upon a fellow prisoner of such nature that he places himself outside the pale of mercy.[8]

Mr. Berry himself suffered sad personal losses with the death of his infant son, March 24, 1868. The Salem Unionist newspaper of the 26th reports that Major Berry and his wife Sarah Isabella, brought the remains of their infant son by boat to The Dalles where a funeral service took place. A Wasco County newspaper of September 17, 1870 reports the funeral of Sarah Isabella, wife of Major M.P. Berry. Her body was laid to rest there in the Catholic Cemetery.

November 14, 1872 court records reflect the marriage of Major M.P. Berry to Jane Eddon in Portland. Jane Eddon was born in England and came to Oregon with her father and sister. She had previously been a maid in the Berry home on Cottage Street between Court and Chemeketa Street. Berry and Eddon had one son Montgomery P. Berry, Jr, in 1874.

March 16, 1874, Berry was appointed by President U.S. Grant as Collector of U.S. Customs in Sitka Alaska. In 1880, he ran for delegate from that district for congress but was not elected. He remained in Sitka where he practiced law. He was a well loved and respected citizen of Sitka at the time of his death December 18, 1898. He is buried in the Sitka National Cemetery. His second wife, Jane Eddon Berry, died June 29, 1896 and is buried with her father John Eddon in the Hobson Whitney Cemetery near Sublimity.

His son, Montgomery Berry, Jr. worked for several years at the State Reform School where he was a cook. His wife Winnie Silvers Berry served as a seamstress. He died in a tragic accident when he contracted blood poisoning while camping at Odell Lake August 3, as reported in the Daily Journal, August 6, 1900. Winnie remarried to Theodore C. Parker, September 25, 1901. She died July 18, 1941.

Number of inmates as of September 14, 1866: 47
Number of employees: 18[9]

Obituary Major Montgomery Pike Berry

The Alaskan Newspaper, Sitka, Alaska December 31, 1898

An old and familiar face has disappeared from our midst in that of Montgomery P. Berry, a gentleman of the old school who will be missed. He departed this life, at the good age of 74 years, on the morning of December the 28th 1:20 am.

He came to Alaska, originally as Collector of Customs for the district, appointed by President U. S. Grant, on March 16, 1874, since which period he has resided amongst us, a well-loved and respected citizen. In 1880 he ran for delegate of the district to Congress against Colonel Ball, by whom he was defeated, principally owing to the fact that before his name had become prominent, the majority of the citizens of Sitka had promised their votes to the Colonel.

Major Berry was a veteran of the Mexican war, but acquired his title from having raised three companies of Federal troops during the civil campaign.

The deceased's son resides at Turner, Marion Co., Oregon, but although many times requested to join his nearest of kin, the Major seemed loath to leave our country.

The funeral took place at 2 pm on Thursday last, the Reverend W. M. Partridge officiating. The volunteer band preceded the procession in accordance with a request made at one time by the deceased. The attendance on the corpse to the grave was large. As a man, Major Berry was whole-souled, independent to an extraordinary degree. He brooked no imposition upon his rights as a man, and a citizen, and has often been known to rebuke both old and young when either attempted an infringement upon those rights. Enemies, we believe he had not, but the reign of his friends was legion and more than one tear shed when the coffin o'er wrapped with "Old Glory" under whose wallings, he had so often fought, slowly wending it's way to the grave, final resting place whence it may perchance rise at the doomsday signal to greet his fellow warriors; who have gone before him; Requiseal in Pace

Berry grave marker at Sitka National Cemetery Sitka, Alaska.. Photo: Carole Healy

"Nothing but iron and rifles hold convicts, and they combined often fail."
Montgomery P. Berry

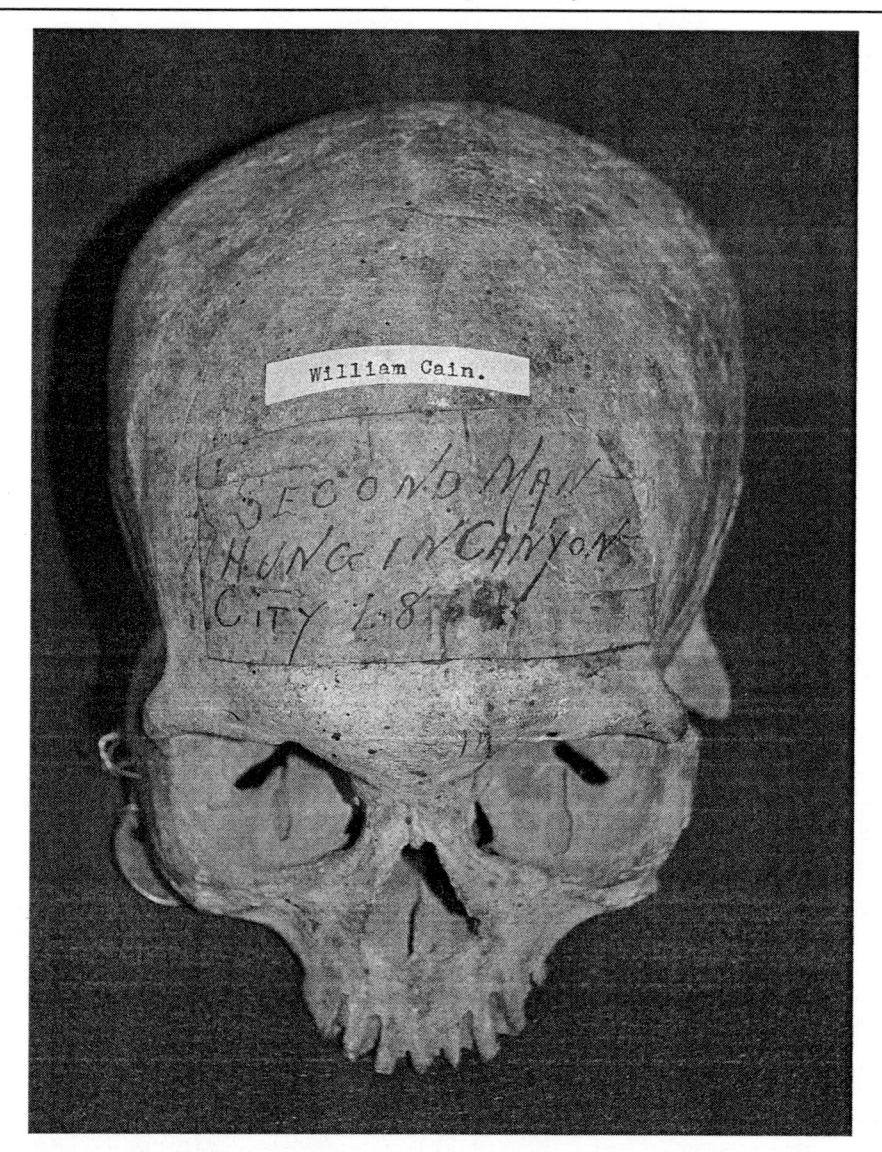

William Kane/Cain 's Skull. Identified as the second man hung in Canyon City. He was the first man hung under Sheriff M.P.Berry's jurisdiction. An earlier hanging of Berry Way occurred in Miners Court. Skull made available for photographing by Grant County Historical Society Museum, Canyon City, OR

Lack of skill by the county hangmen often resulted in decapitation of the body caused by the short drop method of hanging. In 1872 William Marwood developed the long drop technique of hanging which was considered to be more humane. The decapitated skulls were tagged and retained by the Sheriff's office in some jurisdictions.

William H. Watkinds
September 14, 1870-February 14, 1877

William H. Watkinds was born December 7, 1835 in Greencastle, Indiana. He came to Oregon in 1852, crossing the plains with oxen teams The family settled in the Soda Springs area of Linn County.

He was a Democrat, and throughout his life gave much attention to politics. He was trained in saddle and harness making. He and his wife Mary Emily Hixon had a farm in Sublimity where they were living with their three children, Walter Henry, Cora Blanch and Laura.

William H. Watkinds was appointed Superintendent of the Oregon State Penitentiary on September 14, 1870 by Governor Grover and reappointed in 1874 upon Governor Grovers re-election. In 1876 when Governor Grover was elected to the U.S. Senate, Watkinds resigned the office of Superintendent. Representative Men of Oregon reports "during his term of office there passed through his hands nearly $400,000 of public funds and no charge of irregularity in its expenditure has ever been sustained."

Watkinds grave marker at Pioneer Cemetery Salem.
Photo Sue Woodford

In 1873 Superintendent Watkinds lamented about use of the Gardner shackle in a report to the governor, "A great wrong we are compelled to put on the prisoners for want of sufficient walls is the Gardner shackle. We are necessarily compelled to iron them, so they cannot scale the walls. There are prisoners who have worn this instrument of torture, known inside the prison as a man killer until they are broken down in health and constitution. Your excellency ordered a year ago that as few as possible be ironed. This has been complied with, but leaves yet, many ironed down, it is murder of the worst type."

In a quarrel over political issues Watkinds shot Samuel Asahel Clarke, editor of the Statesman Newspaper. Statesman newspaper

In a quarrel over political issues current at the time, he initially horse whipped then shot Samuel Asahel Clarke, editor of the Statesman newspaper. The incident occurred June 14, 1871, in the clothing store of Jim Dalrymple. Clarke sued Watkinds but lost the case. After his resignation, Watkinds, a long time Democrat assisted in founding a newspaper in Salem to voice strongly held political opinions. By 1880, Watkinds moved to Portland managing his saddlery business,. Later he served as Chief of the Portland Police Bureau in 1883 and 1884.[10]

He later returned to Salem and in 1885 his wife Mary Emily was appointed as a matron at the Oregon Insane Asylum where she worked until her death May 25, 1891. William H. Watkinds died November 4, 1889, at the age of 54 years, he is buried in the Salem Pioneer Cemetery with his wife and two children

Number of employees: 21
Number of inmates: 104
Escapes: 3

CONSIGNMENTS SOLICITED.

First St., bet. Main & Salmon, Portland, Og'n.

WM. H. WATKINS,

—Manufacturer and Importer of—

SADDLES, HARNESS,

Bridles, Whips, and Collars,

Saddlery Hardware, Wholesale & Retail.

85 FRONT STREET,

[Corner of Washington,]   Portland, Oregon.

N. B.—Repairing promptly attended to. A good assortment of Concord Stage Harness. Stage Stocks and Lashes of the best quality on hand. Also, a general assortment of Farm Harness on hand.

W.H. Watkinds spelled his name Watkins at times. This advertisement appeared in the City Directory for Portland, Oregon in 1878. One of Watkinds whips is purported to have been used in his attack upon Sam Clarke.
Advertisement courtesy Richard Egan

Plaque installed at OSP when construction was completed Photo: Salem Public Library

"Our State Prison, during the past four years, has been brought up to a much higher standard of discipline and productive industry than was at first anticipated. Four years ago the State was without a tenantable prison. The prison grounds were unimproved and un- drained. Portions of the premises, having been subject to overflow, and remaining at seasons wet, were unhealthy. The prison farm, consisting of one hundred and fifty-seven acres, has been drained, cleared of brush and worthless trees, fenced and reduced to cultivation. A new prison has been built, complete in all appointments, and so substantially constructed that it will stand for centuries." "The efficient management of the Superintendent, Wm. H. Watkinds, Esq., is worthy of high commendation. The care of the health and morals of the prisoners, the success shown in securing to the State cheerful and productive labor, the evident progress made in reformatory discipline all prove the competent and faithful public officer."

Biennial Message of Governor LaFayette Grover to the Legislative Assembly, September 1874, Salem, Oregon, Martin V. Brown, State Printer.

Inmate Dining room OSP Note single light bulbs hung from ceiling on cords
Early Post Card printed in Germany for the Patton Bros. Post Card Hall, Salem, Oregon postmarked 1908

The following is from the booklet Prison Tours and Poems written by Inmate Van Tiffen #4382 in 1906

"We enter the dining room as the last prisoner reaches his place at the table, they all stand in expectant attitudes and as the warden rings the bell to be seated there is a rapid movement, a shuffle of feet, and as the last one takes his place at the table, from far and near we hear the quick clicking of spoons, plates, cups, bowls, etc., and see "flunkies" rushing to and fro.

After a short period of watching, we make a study of the dining room. In one corner, above the floor and commanding a full view of the entire room, we see a cage in which an armed guard is always stationed at mealtime. Other guards are passing the tables, which lay in three rows, or occupy guard stands from which they maintain a lookout.

Radiators are stationed along the walls and during the coldest weather the temperature throughout the entire room (which is about 120 feet long and 70 feet wide at the widest point) is uniform and pleasant. Many large windows admit a plentiful supply of light, and when they are raised, as they always are in the summer time, refreshing breezes are constantly permeating the room.

As the boys finish eating and push their plates slightly towards the center of the table, the noises gradually cease. We turn away for a moment, and as we look again everything is silent and every one waiting expectantly for the bell to ring.

As the bell chimes, those at each table, in prescribed order, arise, and with the signal to leave file from the room."

Benjamin Franklin Burch
February 18, 1877 - October 31, 1878

Benjamin Franklin Burch was born May 2, 1825 in Missouri. His father was Samuel Burch and his mother Eleanor S. Lock. The family emigrated to Oregon in 1845 when Burch was twenty years old. When the Cayuse Indian war broke out Burch enlisted and was made Adjutant of his regiment under Colonels Gilliam and Watters. He served through the Cayuse war of 1847 and 1848 participating in all the battle and was with Colonel Gilliam when the latter was killed. After his Colonels death Burch took charge of the command until it returned to the main body at Walla Walla.[11]

He married Eliza Ann Davidson in 1848 and settled on his donation land claim in Polk county, in a small log cabin.

In the war of 1855-56 Burch served as Captain of Company B First Regiment of Oregon Mounted Riflemen.[12]

In 1857 Burch was elected a member of the State Constitutional Convention and took part in the formation of the State Constitution. As soon as Oregon was admitted to the union, Burch was elected a member of the first legislature. In 1868 he was elected to the state senate and served four years.

Photo OSP

He was appointed by Governor Chadwick to the position of Superintendent of the State Penitentiary and in that capacity he served about two years, 1877 - 1878.

Soon after taking charge of the penitentiary Burch made contracts for the employment of convicts with the Pacific Threshing Machine Co.; J. Stahley, manufacturer of chairs; W. H. Watkinds, Bennett & Harvey, harness makers; Waters and Jackson tanners; J.W. Downer, saddle tree maker; and J.P. Irvine, blacksmith.

Pacific Threshing built a workshop on the prison grounds. J. Stahley remodeled the old bark shed into a chair factory and a new dry house. The blacksmith shop was enlarged and a new forge added. An addition was made to the tannery including a new bark house, some new vats and a bark-mill.

Efforts to build a new brick stockade were thwarted by an existing lease of the brick yard which went beyond Burch's term of office. He did erect a new stockade of lumber. He traded inmate labor cutting logs and running a sawmill to Samuel Bass in exchange for an equal share of lumber. Burch made many needed improvements to the prison physical plant including refurbishing the kitchen.

In his annual report to the governor he states that "wages paid to the guards are fifty dollars per month and I think is reasonable and just."

He was a member of the Southern Methodist church and although not a regular minister often filled the pulpit as a substitute. Burch was a Democrat with strong executive ability. During his service as superintendent at the prison a joint committee appointed by the Legislative Assembly to investigate the affairs of the institution recommended in their report that he be continued in office.

In 1887, President Grover Cleveland appointed Burch as Receiver of the United States Land Office at Oregon City. In that position he is reported to have wisely settled many land claims.

The book *Representative Men of Oregon* describes Burch, "He is of ordinary height and build, plainly dressed, genial and courteous to his friends, and is honest, sincere, and earnest in everything he undertakes. There is a vein of good humor in his composition, and a disposition to relish a good joke."

Burch and his wife had seven children, only two lived to maturity. After the death of their adult son Samuel Burch, the elder Burchs raised his son John Ellis on their farm in Independence.

Burch died March 24, 1893 at the age of 68 years. He is buried in Hill Top Cemetery located on the family donation land claim near Independence. It is noted that while he donated the land for use as a cemetery, his tombstone is one of the smallest and most inconspicuous in the cemetery.

Number of employees: 17
Number of inmates: 145[13]
Escapes:

In 1857 Burch was elected a member of the State Constitutional Convention and took part in the formation of the State Constitution. In 1868 he was elected to the state senate and served four years.

Burch's grave marker at Hill Top Cemetery Independence Photo: Sue Woodford

Asahel Bush
October 31, 1878
December 4, 1882

Asahel Bush was born June 4, 1824 in Westfield, Massachusetts. He was appointed as Superintendent of the Oregon State Penitentiary in 1878. While living in Westfield, Mass., he studied law and was admitted to the bar of Massachusetts in 1850. Bush is best known as a pioneer journalist and banker in Salem having founded the Oregon Statesman newspaper in 1853 where he published the paper until he sold it in 1861. In 1867 he entered the banking business as a member of the firm of Ladd & Bush. His partner was W.S. Ladd until Mr. Ladd sold his interest in 1877. Mr. Bush's various business interests included Salem Flouring Mills, Salem Woolen Mills, Salem Foundry, Oregon Steam Navigation Company and others.

Photo courtesy Oregon State Library

He was a Democrat who took an active part in the welfare of his party in Oregon. He served as a member of the Democratic State Central Committee for several years. Asahel Bush while publishing his newspaper the Oregon Statesman in the 1850s expressed strongly worded editorials favoring a "white only" state. He was given to expressing vitriolic personal comments about people who's opinions differed from his. A local Congregational minister who officiated at the wedding of African American citizens was one of his targets as was Colonel Shiel, Attorney, Congressman, and Territorial Auditor, who differed with Bush on political issues.[14] The Oregon Historical Society reports, "Bush was visibly racist and defended slavery, but he also condemned Southern secession and supported the Union during the Civil War."

Bush was active in politics as a member of an influential group of Salem Democrats which favored the location of the territorial capital in Salem and favored the prohibition of slavery in Oregon. Bush owned a Rolls Royce driven by a chauffeur and a private railroad car, used for travel across country to the east coast. He reportedly did not like to use money that had been handled by others so visited his bank daily for clean bills.[15] Bush wanted the position of Superintendent of OSP because he believed he could significantly reduce the cost to the taxpayer, of housing

Bush grave marker Pioneer Cemetery Salem
Photo Sue Woodford

inmates. Bush volunteered to serve without pay for the first two years of his appointment to OSP. He cut costs from $3.20 per week, per inmate to $1.96 per week, per inmate. In his 1880 Biennial Report he stated " I had long been of the opinion that the penitentiary was costing the state too much, and was largely influenced to accept the appointment, for the purpose of ascertaining whether or not this opinion was well founded. The result you have, and I am now ready to give place to another when you shall appoint." It appears that he was satisfied that he had done all that he could to improve the physical plant, reduce costs, improve the health of the prisoners, and attend to the spiritual wants of the prisoners by the ministry of Reverend J. L. Parrish who preached on the first Sunday of each month.

During Bush's tenure as superintendent, important construction at the Oregon State Penitentiary occurred as well as many repairs having been made. He reported, "the boilers used for warming the prison and workshops have been in use about twenty five years, were originally in the old Willamette steamboat "Canemah" and are considered not quite safe." He further reported, "We have not found employment for all the convicts, and more or less of them are at all times idle in the cells." "If we could find employment for all the surplus convicts at fifty cents per day, the prison would pay considerably more than all its expenses." The night guard was being paid forty dollars per month and threatened to quit if the wages were not raised and were so done by Bush. Regarding his own position, Bush stated, "I regard the office of superintendent as an unnecessary one, except as inspector or commissioner, and I would recommend it be abolished and a board of inspectors substituted, to consist of three members, with salary of two hundred dollars per year, each, which would be sufficient compensation."

Bush was united in marriage to Eugenia Zieber in October 1854. They had four children. Eugenia Bush died, September 11, 1863, age 30. Asahel Bush died December 24, 1913. He was 89. He is buried in the Pioneer Cemetery in Salem.

Number of employees: 16
Number of inmates: 180[16]
Escapes: 2

He reportedly did not like to use money that had been handled by others so visited his bank daily for clean bills.[15]

Bush House — Bush Pasture Park Salem landmark Photo Sue Woodford

Julius Augustus Stratton
December 4, 1882- October 14, 1884

Julius A. Stratton was born in Jefferson County Indiana October 13, 1844 to Curtis P. Stratton and Lavinia Fitch Stratton. He was one of twelve children. The Stratton family moved to Oregon in 1854 in a covered wagon, when Julius was 10 years old. They relocated to Salem from the Umpqua valley in July 1861. At that time Julius began work for the Oregon Statesman newspaper where he learned the printers trade. He worked at the newspaper until 1865 continuing part time until his graduation from Willamette University in 1879. He studied law and was admitted to the bar in 1871. In 1882 he was appointed as Superintendent of the Oregon State Penitentiary.

In 1883 a large quantity of brick was required for completion of the Insane Asylum and the penitentiary was directed to supply the bricks. Stratton had the inmate shop enlarged to allow more inmates to work on the brick project. He also added twenty two cells over the north wing and rebuilt the stockade in the yard. Stratton's predecessor Asahel Bush had negotiated a contract with Goldsmith and Lowenberg of the Northwest Foundry Corporation for the manufacture of stoves.

Photo by permission, Catherine Stratton with a copy of his recollections, written in 1913

Inmates were paid forty cents per day for work in the foundry. Stratton reported, "The results of the employment of the convicts under the existing contract so far are most encouraging. It accustoms them to habits of industry, without which I think any efforts at reform are likely to prove futile; enables them to learn a trade by which they can, when discharged, support themselves by honest labor, and is remunerative to the state." Stratton learned the value of hard work at a young age.

He was also concerned with the safety of the inmates and staff. He had the machine which supplied gas to the prison moved from the prison basement to a small brick building a safe distance from the prison. He also moved the bake oven and laundry from the basement to buildings erected outside, thus diminishing the risk of fire as well as improving the atmosphere of the prison. In the annual report, Stratton stated that a change should be made in the law relating to the salary of the Superintendent." The present compensation is not enough to command all the time of a competent man, and is more than enough for an inspector. I think, however, that the office may be dispensed with altogether and the duties devolved upon the warden without detriment to the service."

He moved from Oregon in February 1888 to Seattle where he was appointed Prosecuting Attorney of King County and in 1890 Judge of the Superior Court of King County by Governor Ferry.
He married Martha L. Powell in 1889, she died in 1895. In August 1900 in Victoria, B.C., he wed Laura M. Adams, an accomplished musician.

The couple had one son, Julius Adams Stratton who enjoyed an illustrious career as a scientist. Graduating from MIT, he joined the faculty there and later served both as vice president and president of MIT. He was one of the first members of MIT's radiation laboratory where major research in U.S. development of radar was carried out. He served as expert consultant on radar to U.S. secretary of war during WW II.

Julius Augustus Stratton died September 23, 1924. He was 80 years old. He is interred in Bonny Watson Memorial Park Mausoleum in Seattle, Washington. Stratton's parents are interred in Salem Pioneer Cemetery beside his brother Riley Stratton former Oregon Supreme Court Justice.

Number of employees: 18
Number of inmates September 7, 1884: 256
Escapes: 6
Attempted Escapes: 14[17]

Julius Stratton's son Julius Adams Stratton served as president of MIT

The old wall at OSP. A new wall was built in the 1950s outside the old wall, and the old wall was torn down, increasing the size of the prison yard. Photo OSP

George Collins
October 14, 1884 - February 1, 1887

George O. Collins was born July 20, 1834 in Eastport, Maine George learned the brick laying trade at an early age. In 1865 he headed west to California by steamer via the Nicaragua route.

He initially landed in San Francisco where he married Jennie Hamilton. They took the steamer for Portland, Oregon where they met Father Waller a pioneer missionary who advised Collins to settle in Salem. In Salem he met H.C. Myers, also from Maine and they formed a partnership in contracting and building.

The History of Oregon reports , "In the spring of 1869 George Collins accepted an offer made by Major M. P. Berry, who was the superintendent of the Oregon State Penitentiary to take charge as warden of the convict labor at the state brick yard, where he was employed until the fall of 1870, when the Watkinds - Berry transition occurred. In the fall of 1873, he returned to Salem where he was employed as superintendent of construction on the Oregon state house, continuing until the appropriation was exhausted."

He then leased the state brickyard and convict labor, and made brick for the Oregon Insane Asylum, the Scotch mill, and for the general market. He continued in this until 1882, when the administration again became Republican, when he was offered and accepted, the position of first warden of the State penitentiary, under J. A. Stratton, Superintendent.

In 1883 during a revolt among the convicts, Collins very nearly lost his life. By coolness and self possession, reenforced by other assistants, four convicts were killed and the others brought under subjection. He continued as warden until 1884 when, upon the resignation of Stratton, Collins was appointed superintendent, which office he filled until February 1, 1887. He, too then resigned and continued his former occupation of brick manufacturing.

Photo OSP

House built by George Collins 301 Church St. Moved to 1340 Chemeketa St. NE. Salem, Photo: Sue Woodford

During his tenure as Superintendent, Mr. Collins recommended the purchase of a Gatling gun, at a cost of $1,200, for the new towers.[18]

Collins built a home at 301 Church Street in Salem. George Collins died 25 February 1913, at the home of his daughter Esther Collins Chatten in Portland. He was 76 years old. His wife died February 5, 1907. He is buried in the Lee Mission Cemetery in the Old section (153-4) with his wife and son George Collins, Jr.

Number of employees: 22
Highest number of inmates: 298
Average number of inmates: 278
Escapes: 2[19]

Following Collins' resignation as superintendent, Officer George Clow served as an acting superintendent from February 1, 1877 to March 13, 1888, along with his regular work as a warden/guard. During the summer of 1887, one million, one hundred thirty two thousand bricks were manufactured in the OSP brick yard.

George Collins seated on wagon, standing are: Dr. McNary, Jasper (Jap) Minto, displaying birds from a hunting expedition. Photo Salem Public Library

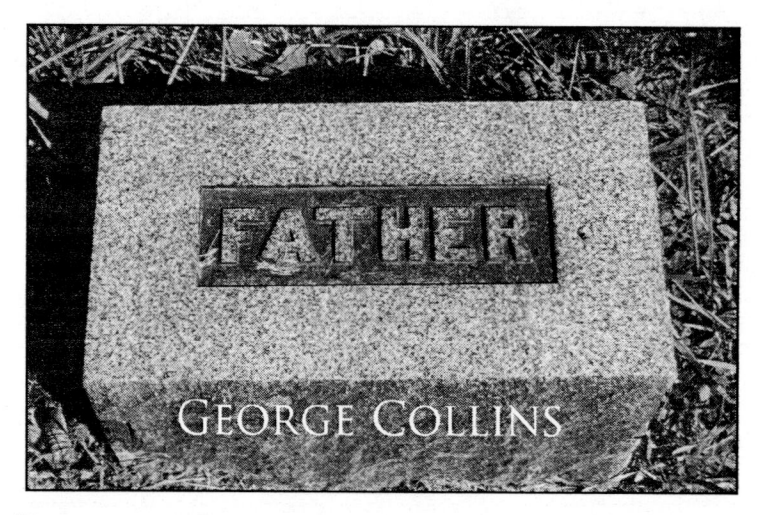

Collins grave marker at Lee Mission Cemetery Salem Photo: Sue Woodford

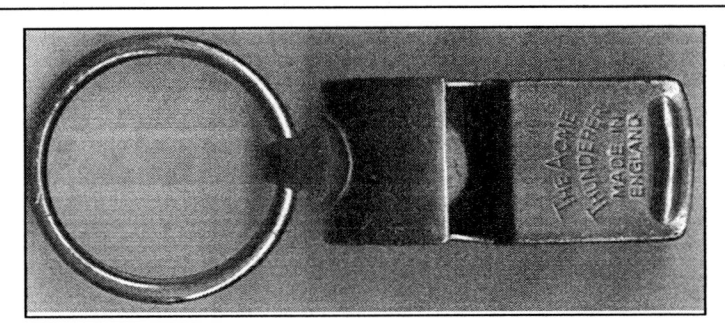

Acme Thunderer Whistle used by OSP guards until the 1980's as warning devices. Photo: Sue Woodford

Rules and Regulations for Assistant Wardens Rule 11: The Assistant Warden shall be required to keep with him a time-piece with the prison time, and also a whistle with which to call up the prisoners, ten minutes before the usual time of leaving the yard, that they may prepare themselves to be lined up, two and two, with the heavy ironed men in front, ready to march at the tap of the prison bell. He shall count the prisoners, and before starting for the enclosures, blow his whistle twice, as a signal to the guards that he is ready to march, and they may leave their posts. This rule shall be observed in all cases, except at the approach of a storm, or when the work in hand requires a delay not prejudicial to the safe return of the prisoners. October 1, 1870 Biennial Report W. H. Watkinds, Superintendent

Early post card of Oregon Insane Asylum. The building was later transferred to the Department of Corrections to serve as it's headquarters. It is now known as the Dome Building located at 2575 Center St. SE in Salem. There are a network of tunnels under this building connecting it with the State Hospital J building, Oregon State Prison and at one time to the Oregon State Capitol building. A narrow gauge railroad allowed the easy transport of goods between buildings, patients were also moved from one place to another by way of the tunnels, out of public view.

George S. Downing (top hat center). Photo includes Wardens, Guards and family members. Note that the guards hold rifles and canes - equipment used in safeguarding the institution

George S. Downing
March 13, 1888 - March 9, 1895

George Sylvester Downing was born October 28, 1834 in Pennsylvania to Alexander Downing and Elizabeth Burns. Downing emigrated to Oregon in 1853. He worked in the office of a former superintendent (1882 - 1884) Judge Julius Stratton, studying law. He was admitted to practice law in the courts of Oregon in 1882.

A biographical sketch in the Book of Remembrance states, "When Mr. Downing undertook this prison work, he found much dissatisfaction among the convicts and at once introduced music and singing, as well as literary entertainment among them, thus relieving the tedium of prison life, to some extent."

A substantial and attractive steel bar fence was constructed across the front of the main building. The entrance gate through this fence is operated by hydraulic water-pressure. The fence including the gate was constructed under contract at the cost of $3,715. The fence is 432 feet long. Two wood buildings were constructed one for a store house and one for a soap factory, also constructed an iron armory or safe for the better protection of our firearms and ammunition not in use."

Superintendent Downing recommended the addition of sky lights in the roof of the prison. He asked that the water towers be removed from the roof and a tower be constructed apart from the main building. He requested, "The erection of a small woolen mill at the penitentiary to be run and operated by convict labor for the purpose of manufacturing blankets and cloth for the use of convicts." He stated, "We have United States prisoners and small boys that cannot be used in the foundry that could be employed in such an enterprise." At that time convicts were accepted at OSP at age 16. [20]

He also recommended construction of a building to be used for hospital purposes, a portion of which could be for a reformatory school, "where young criminals could receive moral and religious training." Superintendent Downing was a deacon in the Campbellite Christian church. He placed a high value on the chapel services conducted at least every two weeks. He recommended hiring a full time chaplain.

" Mr. Downing was a member of the Masonic Lodge, organized the Grange and served as State Master, served eight years as Chief Marshall for the State Agricultural Society during state fairs. He was a familiar figure riding about on horseback with his red sash across his shoulder. He was a Democrat."

During the time that Downing was superintendent, his family occupied the front portion of the front wing of the penitentiary, and the office and reception room was in the rear portion of the wing, the entrance to the rotunda being through double iron doors from the office.

He was married three times, first to Missouri Evans who died in 1865, second to Mary Evans Smith, his first wife's sister who died February 22, 1880, third to Elizabeth A. Rossiter. Elizabeth died March 3, 1932. George Downing died November 7, 1916. He was 82. He is interred in the Mt. Crest Abbey Mausoleum in Salem,

Number of employees: 25
Number of inmates (1891): 277
Highest number of inmates: 333
Escapes: 1
Cost per day per inmate: 13.07 Cents per day[21]

"At that time convicts were accepted at OSP at age 16." [20]

Downing's marker at Mt. Crest Abbey Mausoleum in Salem.

Photo Sue Woodford

A kinder more gentle time at OSP, on the surface

George Downing's wife and children playing croquet on the lawn at OSP

George Downing (fifth from left) with his family

Andrew Nathan Gilbert
March 04, 1895 - 1899

Andrew Gilbert was born in Grand View, Illinois in 1840 to James Gilbert and Margaret Hurst. He was educated in Illinois and Indiana and emigrated to Oregon over the Old Mullen Trail at the end of the civil war in 1866.

Arriving in Salem, he engaged in the boot and shoe business. His first connection with the Oregon State Penitentiary was as a clerk in charge of the shoe department. He was engaged in a variety of other business interests in Salem and Harrisburg. His wife's father, David McCully was the founder of Harrisburg. He participated in the organization of the Republican party, was elected city treasurer of Salem in 1870, 1874.

In 1876 was elected to represent his county in the state legislature and in 1882 was again elected to the legislature. He became Post Master of Salem under President Harrison. Governor Lord appointed him to serve as superintendent of the state penitentiary, a position he held for four years. He carried out the wishes of the Governor that, "there must be the influence of moral forces upon the inmates character and regular employment upon his habits in order to effect reformation."

A major concern of Gilbert was the prison sanitation system. Inmates became ill with malaria and other fevers which the prison physician thought was caused by sewer gasses seeping into the cells through the sinks plumbing. The prison sewers were wooden boxes one hundred and fifty feet in length, accumulating rottenness without traps. Gilbert wanted them replaced. He also noted in the biennial report that while $800 was appropriated for inmate bathtubs, there was no bath house or suitable place for the tubs. Existing bathing facilities consisted of four wooden boxes in the prison engine room. The boxes were to be used to bathe one hundred men every Saturday. [22]

Gilbert replaced the hand made, vermin breeding, wooden bedsteads in the prison hospital with regular iron hospital bedsteads with good spring mattresses. The former window curtains made of wall paper and flour sacks were replaced with modern blinds. The leaky useless bathtub was replaced with a new one.

There were only two female prisoners and Gilbert recommended that legislative action be taken to have the women housed in the State Reform School under supervision of matrons.

Gilbert praised the work of the volunteer preacher C. Kate Smith who had been preaching one Sunday a month. At his direction, religious services were held each Sunday. He made a change to exclude visitors at the religious services. The previous administration had allowed ten and twenty women and children to attend services with four hundred convicts. Gilbert thought this to be an unsafe practice.

In the summer of 1895 one million bricks were manufactured by the prison for construction of the state sewer.

Gilbert voiced the opinion that, "inmates have been contented and obedient, rather preferring to be at work in the shops than to be idle in their cells."

He died July 14, 1923. He was 83. He and his wife and daughter are interred in the Mt Crest Abbey Mausoleum, Salem. He was married to Estelle McCully Gilbert, April 27, 1871. She died July 14, 1933. They had three children, Ray David, Henry Warren and Agnes Gilbert Schucking. His residence was located at 295 North Liberty Street in Salem.

Number of Employees: 25
Number of inmates (1897): 368
Escapes: 0[23]

Prison sanitation in the 1890s was deplorable. Sewer gases seeped into cells sickening prisoners and mosquitoes spread malaria. The hospital was also vermin-infested and Gilbert addressed these conditions.

Oregon State Hospital was constructed of bricks made by inmates at the prison. This photo is of a ground breaking ceremony. Photo OSP

Rules and Regulations for Assistant Wardens Rule 10: He shall see that the guard in charge of the brick yard gate shall count the prisoners when they leave the prison enclosures, and also upon their return to the same, calling back the count to the Assistant Warden. He shall count the prisoners as they enter the brick yard. He shall keep a record of the number of prisoners detailed for labor outside the brick yard, and the guard in charge of such prisoners shall report to him the number, when returned from such duty. After the prisoners are upon the brick yard, he shall put them to work as the Superintendent of the brick making shall direct, unless the same shall, in his opinion, endanger their safe keeping. He shall also see that the said Superintendent shall hold no conversation with the prisoners, nor the latter among themselves, except in a low tone.
Biennial Report October 1, 1870, Superintendent W. H. Watkinds

Meier and Frank Company.

Established 1857.   Incorporated 1892.

185 & 187 First St.
184 to 194 Second St.
229 to 235 Taylor St.

Portland, Or. July 5, 1898.

A. N. Gilbert, Esq.,

  Supt. Oregon State Penitentiary, Salem, Or.

Dear Sir:-

  Regarding your order for 200 yards striped material, we are unable to procure the exact material and enclose sample of the nearest which we offer at 18¢ per yard. It is somewhat superior to the sample you sent us and, if it will answer your purpose we will order it from the East immediately. In case you order, kindly return sample, and oblige

  Yours very truly,

Striped fabric was ordered from Meier and Frank Company for inmate Uniforms. _{Oregon State Archives}

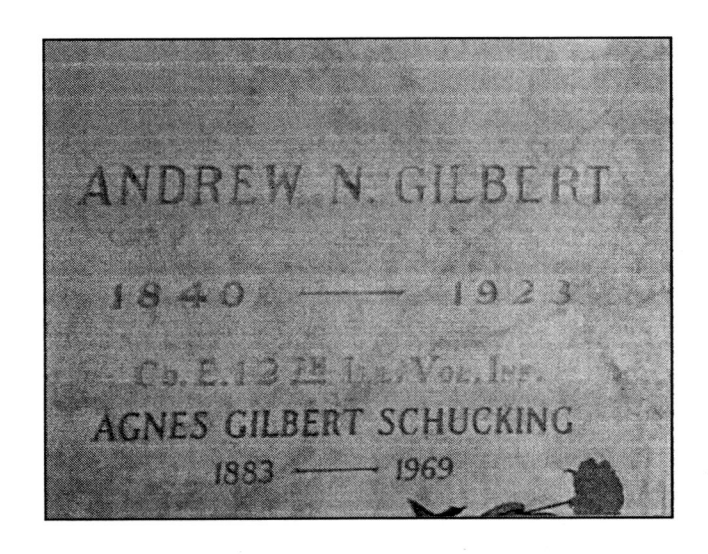

ANDREW N. GILBERT
1840 — 1923
Co. E. 137 Ind. Vol. Inf.
AGNES GILBERT SCHUCKING
1883 — 1969

Gilbert Marker at Mt. Crest Abbey Mausoleum
Photo Sue Woodford

Joseph Daniel Lee:
April 1, 1899 - April 1, 1903

Joseph Daniel Lee was born July 27, 1848 to Nicholas Lee and Sarah Hopper, near the present site of Monmouth, Oregon. As an adult he was a man of striking appearance being six feet six inches tall and weighing over 200 pounds. He married Eliza Alice Witten on May 19, 1872. Four children were born to this union.

He was elected as a representative from Polk County in 1878. He also served as Postmaster in Dallas. Lee had business interests in Independence, Dallas and Portland. He assisted in obtaining subscriptions for construction of a trolly line from Portland to Oregon City and in construction of Columbia University now known as Portland State University.

When a major depression occurred in Portland in 1895, Lee downsized his business property and took a job with the state as a deputy clerk in the municipal court of Portland. After his term expired he was appointed as a reading clerk at a special session of the legislature in 1898.

Photo OSP

Joseph Lee was appointed Superintendent of the Oregon State Penitentiary by Governor T.T. Geer, April 1, 1899 and served until April 1, 1903. Superintendent Lee's strengths were as a business manager rather than as an experienced penologist.

Lee built a modern dairy farm on the prison grounds. He improved sanitary conditions, equipped and installed a fine modern prison kitchen and made nearly all the preparations for the equipment of the new community inmate dining room. The reason he did not install the dining room was that the room intended for the purpose had a ceiling built too low. A high ceiling was required for the guard to adequately patrol the room from an elevated catwalk.

He made many improvements in the operations of OSP and introduced the Bertillion System of inmate measurement and identification but failed to recognize the need for proper custody classification of inmates.

He did not separate Harry Tracy, a renowned escape artist, from Tracy's partner in crime, David Merrill, but housed them together in the same cell at OSP. Harry Tracy and David Merrill escaped from the Oregon State Penitentiary on June 9, 1902. One of the longest manhunts ever was undertaken to capture these two escapees. Lee appeared deeply affected by the escape of the two inmates and the subsequent death and harm done in the wake of this criminal episode. The guards killed in the escape were Frank Ferrell, Thurston Jones, and Baily T. Tiffany. The corpse of David Merrill was returned to the prison July 17, 1902 and Harry Tracy's corpse was returned on August 9, 1902 and the rewards for each collected.[24]

J. D. Lee's presence January 31, 1902 at the hanging of John Wade and B.H. Dalton, two convicted felons, was noted in the Morning Oregonian February 1, 1902. By 1904 all hangings would occur at the prison in spite of Lee's objections voiced in an article January 31, 1902 Portland Evening Telegram..

Joseph Lee was a noted Oregon pioneer and developer. He purchased the property and platted the city of Lake Oswego. Joseph Lee died November 22, 1927 at his residence at 4828 32nd Ave SE, Portland, OR. He was 79. He is interred in the Lincoln Cemetery in Portland

Employees: 25
Inmates: 368
Escapes: 2

The Escape of Harry Tracy and David Merrill June 9, 1902

"The outbreak was entirely unexpected, and under the circumstances could not be prevented. The two men were supplied with rifles from the outside, probably brought over the wall during the night and secreted in the place where tools were kept in the foundry, and where the prisoners secured them. This would be possible during the night, as there is but one guard inside the yard at night. I was not in the prison when the outbreak occurred, but came soon after, and have directed the pursuit. I have sent for a brace of bloodhounds from Walla Walla and they should arrive at 11 tomorrow, when the trail will be followed and the murderers run to earth. It is an awful affair and I will never rest until I run the fiends down." Superintendent J. D. Lee[25]

Lee grave marker at Lincoln Cemetery in Portland. Photo: Sue Woodford

DOES NOT CARE FOR ALL THE HANGINGS

STATE PENITENTIARY IS NO PLACE FOR SUCH A MONOPOLY.

This Is the Opinion of Superintendent Lee, of Oregon's State Prison, Who Believes That the Influence Upon Prisoners Would Be Prejudicial to Discipline.

Superintendent J. D. Lee, of the Oregon State Penitentiary, is no believer in a monopoly of executions at the State Prison, as is the practice, fixed by law, in some states. On the contrary, he sees many objections to the system.

"One of the essentials to discipline is good conduct, as well as moral reform," said Mr. Lee this morning, in discussing legal executions and the desire of some to have all hangings at the State Penitentiary. "Is favorable environment. Hangings at the State Penitentiary would have a decidedly baleful influence on the prisoners, in my opinion. Executions by the law, instead of striking terror into the hearts of hardened criminals, would probably only arouse the demon within them and the result would be prejudicial to discipline, to say the least. Prisoners are controlled by influence as much as force. If hangings were conducted at the penitentiary, the prisoners would necessarily know of it. Every execution would divert their thoughts from their work and fix their attention upon the victim of the gallows. On some it might have a beneficial effect, but as to the majority I believe it would only serve as a firebrand to stir up their baser natures and increase their thrist for revenge.

"Still another objection to a monopoly of executions at the State Prison is the danger attending the transportation of condemned prisoners from the remoter sections of the state. It would be an easy matter for friends or confederates of murderers to effect their rescue and assist in their escape in sections of the state where much staging is necessary.

"I believe in executions without publicity, and also believe it would be a good thing perhaps to have a central prison, where such executions should be conducted. Such a prison should be located in Portland, the electric chair should supplant the gallows and no date for executions should be fixed. It would be better for the public not to know anything of executions until after they are over."

Portland Evening Telegram Newspaper January 31, 1902

I believe it would only serve as a firebrand to stir up their baser natures and increase their thirst for revenge.

J. D. Lee regarding plan to move hangings to the state prison

PRISON OFFICIALS LOOKOUT

Suspicious Characters Attempt to Gain Admittance Inside the Walls

The officials at the Oregon penitentiary are wrought up over what they believe to have been an attempt to smuggle arms or explosives into the institution. The Southern Pacific bridge carpenters are at work on the switch and bridge inside the walls, and on Friday afternoon two strangers appeared along the track. The boss carpenter ordered the intruders away, and, as they were leaving, noticed that one of them carried a package under his arm, but concealed by his coat. He at once notified the prison officials, but, as the strangers were not guilty of a crime, it was passed over, and nothing more was thought of the matter until today, when the same men again attempted to steal past the workmen. They were carrying bundles under their clothing, and, from the description of the men, the officers are certain they are ex-convicts, who are determined to assist men on the inside to escape. The most probable theory, and the one that is giving the officers the most concern, is that the packages contained dynamite, and an attempt had been planned with that explosive. The city and county officers have been notified to keep a strict lookout for suspicious characters, and if they are found around the penitentiary again they will be taken in charge.

April 9, 1903 Journal Newspaper

Before Fingerprints were used as a common identifier Bertillion method was used.

Alphonse Bertillion's identification process developed in 1893 measured the following:

Height
Stretch: Length of body from left shoulder to right middle finger when arm is raised.
Bust: Length of torso from head to seat, taken when seated.
Length of head: Crown to forehead.
Width of head: Temple to temple.
Length of right ear.
Length of left foot.
Length of left middle finger.
Length of left cubit: Elbow to tip of middle finger.
Width of cheeks
Length of left little finger.

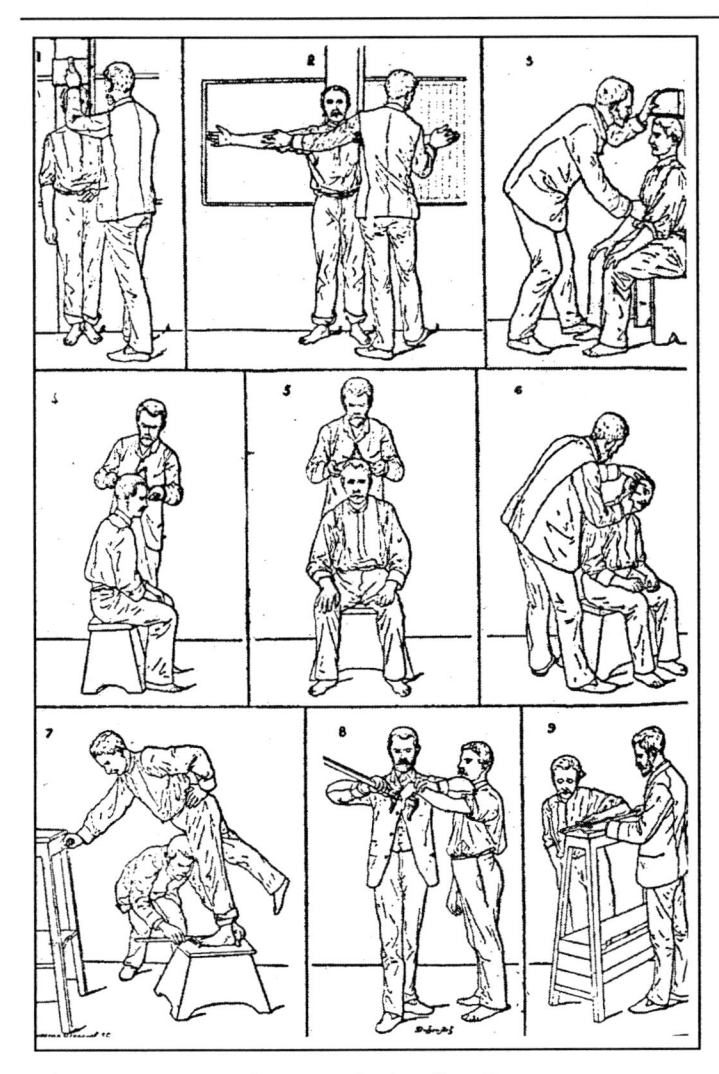

Before Fingerprint ID there was the Bertillion System

The Bertillion system utilized body measurements, individual markings, tattoos, scars and personality characteristics to classify inmate records. This system made it easy to sift through a large number of records quickly to narrow the pool of possible people and then compare the person with a photograph. The system was limited and eventually was replaced with fingerprinting.[26]

The first systematic use of fingerprints occurred in the New York State Prison system in 1903.

In 1909 the Bureau of Criminal Identification was established at the Oregon State Penitentiary. A general order stated, "All incoming prisoners will be fingerprinted."

The Oregon State Penitentiary identification officer took and maintained fingerprint and mug shot records. These records were housed in the prison records office.

Joe Murray established and maintained the records/identification section of OSP from 1911 until his retirement in 1953 at age 70.

Prior to 1911 mug shots of inmates were taken by the prison druggist as assigned by the Superintendent.

Old A Block completed in 1901 dismantled in 1947, replaced with E Block

OSP Hospital Room 1915   Lee added modern window blinds and metal cots for hospital beds

Oregon State Penitentiary gallows used for legally ordered executions before the installation of the gas chamber in 1938. Hangings occurred January 29, 1904 to October 30, 1931. Pictured is Joe Murray, OSP Records Officer — Bertillion expert. Photo OSP

The death penalty for first degree murder was adopted in Oregon by statute in 1864. County Sheriffs had the authority to carry out these executions. However, the executions became a source of embarrassment because of the circus like atmosphere that prevailed.

In 1903 the Oregon Legislature, in order to restrict public attendance at executions, amended the law to require executions be carried out at the Oregon State Penitentiary in Salem.[27]

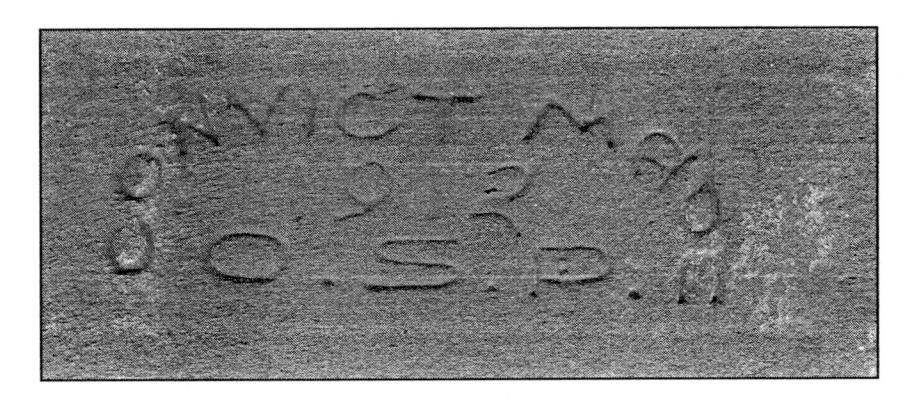

Bricks made by inmates in the prison brick yard were so marked. "Convict Made 1912 O.S.P." This brick was used in the construction of the columns of the old Oregon State Capitol building. Photo Sue Woodford

Hangman: William E. Lamb, born September 11, 1857, died January 5, 1937, Lamb was employed at OSP sixteen years as a guard. During that time he hanged fourteen men. Stephen A. Stone, Oregon Memorabilia, 1967 Parkstone Co., Photo Stephen A. Stone with permission

Oregon State Penitentiary 1899

Charles W. James
April 1, 1903 to May 6, 1912

Charles W. James was born March 5, 1851 in Green county, Missouri and emigrated to Baker, Oregon in 1867 with his parents. His father Winfrey James was a physician in Baker City. Charles was employed as a school teacher. After his marriage he farmed and raised stock. He sold the farm and moved to Baker City where he owned a drug store. He was appointed post master and served in that position for ten years. In 1893 he served as Vice President of the Baker City National Bank. By 1903 he had moved to Salem where he was appointed as superintendent of Oregon State Penitentiary, April 1

According to the OSP publication "Lend a Hand", the Oregon Prisoners Aid Society was founded April 1903, at the start of the James administration. The Society known as OPAS was not only influential in the "Lend a Hand" publication but other measures within the prison as well. The OPAS and other outside interests made demands and held the James administration accountable for the entire prison community. This outside influence hampered the prison authority and was not viewed favorably. A fire occurred in the superintendents cottage on May 2, 1908. Newspaper reports indicted the presence of Mrs. Rosalia James, daughters Myrta and Irene and Irene's husband Tom Wilson as being unharmed during the fire. Tom Wilson was a clerk at OSP. The fire was due to faulty wiring and the cottage was rebuilt with inmate labor.

Photo OSP

In 1904, James purchased a camera for $50.00 to take photos of the prisoners as per Oregon Statute. The photography assignment was given to the prison druggist who took the photos at a cost of fifteen cents each. Prior to this time outside photographers took the photos at a cost of $1.00 each.

Superintendent James recommended the abolition of capital punishment and supported a bill to that effect introduced by Senator Hal D. Patton. Governor Oswald West while expressing no opinion also appeared to favor the amendment. Sixteen months later, May 2, 1912, Governor West fired superintendent James citing reasons of economy. The two appeared to differ in their opinion of how many inmates ought to be used in trustee or honor positions.

The Governor initially tried to place James on a leave of absence hoping he would resign. James offered to work without pay if all other employees did the same. The Governor rejected James proposal and fired him along with Chaplains Bauer, Moore and Supervising Engineer Larrabee, Head Farmer W. J. White and Matron Lillian Curtis (wife of F. H. Curtis, who replaced James)

It was reported that Governor West resisted firing James outright for fear of bringing disapproval upon himself of Senator Chamberlain, at whose instance James was retained. Later it was learned that the Governor

Front row far left: Hamilton Curtis, third from left; Superintendent C.W. James. Curtis was appointed to replace James when the governor removed James[28]

did not have the authority to suspend James with pay or to place him on leave with pay and that the only way he could get rid of him was to fire him outright. It was also determined that the Governor did not have the authority to terminate other prison employees. That authority was vested in the Superintendent.

In 1905, legislation was enacted providing sentencing guidelines for felonies for indeterminate periods (bench parole) and authority was given to the Governor to parole prisoners. The superintendent of the State Penitentiary was to keep a record of all paroles and discharges. The State Parole Board, consisting of three members, was established in 1911. The Governor appointed two of the members while the superintendent of the Oregon State Penitentiary held the third position. The board investigated all cases where prisoners were confined under indeterminate sentences and reported parole recommendations to the Governor. The Parole Board was required to keep in communication with all persons released on parole.

The Governor wanted to place warden F. H. Curtis, James assistant, in charge of the prison and abolish the position of superintendent as a money saving plan. He blamed the legislature for reducing the prison appropriation by $10,000. By eliminating the superintendent and staff positions he claimed he could save $5,000. This would enable him to complete his term as Governor without any financial deficiency.
James left the position and was replaced by Frank Curtis.

In later years James moved to Nye Beach with his wife Rosalie Boyd James and daughter Myrta James. He and Rosalie had five children; Myrta, Arthur, Viola, Irena, and Roscoe James. He was living at Nye Beach in Newport in 1930 with his daughter Myrta after the death of his wife Rosalia January 15, 1930. We have been unable to learn the date of Charles James death or the whereabouts of his interment.

Number of inmates: 479 1911, 375 1912   (Capacity listed as 430)[29]
Number of employees: 50 (27 staff are pictured in the photo)[30]
Number of Escapes: 20

Superintendent James recommended the abolition of capital punishment and supported a bill to that effect introduced by Senator Hal D. Patton. Governor Oswald West while expressing no opinion also appeared to favor the amendment. Sixteen months later, May 2, 1912, Governor West fired superintendent James citing reasons of economy.

Oregon Reform School also know as State Training School for Boys changed to Prison Farm Annex in 1929

CONFINED	DISCIPLINARY RECORD	GUARD/WARDEN	RELEASED
	Farley Hunt # 6798		
9-12-13	Eight hours at door - Destroying tools-	Golden	
9-11-14	Ten hours at door - Shooting craps-	Benjen	
10-10-16	Placed in dungeon - Escaping-	Sherwood	10-20-16
10-23-16	Placed in bull pen-	Sherwood	11-9-16
2-16-18	Placed on blacklist - playing cards		2-27-18
11-6-17	Escaped		
11-15-17	Returned and placed in stripes		
2-25-18	Four hours at door-Gambling		
2-26-18	Four hours at door-Gambling		
	Oscar Herman # 6922		
12-11-12	Six hours at door - Disobeying orders -	Abbott	
6-15-15	Released from trusty force-good time taken having cigarettes and money in possession	Warden Minto	
	C. E. Hall # 6754		
5-14-14	Eight hours at door -Profanity	Snodgrass	
10-29-24	Ten hours at door - Disobedience	Snodgrass	
10-30-14	Sixteen hours at door - Refused to work and cursed guard	Snodgrass	
1-8-15	Six hours at door-called guard liar	Abbott	
3-22-15	Six hours at door - Electric extension in cell	Johnson	
10-20-15	Eight days in dungeon - Abusive Language	Buscik	
1-14-16	Eight hours at door - Smoking Cigarettes	Groves	
2-27-17	Eight hours at door - Smoking Cigarettes	Oleson	
	Otto Hill # 6586		
9-9-14	Placed in solitary - Escaping	Benjen	10-12-24
	Otto Hooker # 7198		
12-9-14	Ten hours at door - Refused to work	Abbott	
2-8-15	Six hours at door - Barked like a dog	Groves	
	George Harris # 7066		
12-3-16	Three in dungeon- Fighting	Burkhart	

Early disciplinary records of OSP inmates
Oregon State Archives

During James tenure as Superintendent of OSP, Franz Edmund Creffield was one of the more notorious inmates housed there. He was the leader of a religious sect (Holy Rollers), mostly women, in Corvallis. Creffield married Maud Hurt and later was sentenced to prison for adultery. After his release from prison, Creffield was killed by George Mitchell, brother of one of the young women followers. Mitchell was acquitted of the murder. Esther Mitchell then killed her brother July 12, 1906. Esther Mitchell said, "I killed George because he had killed an innocent man and ruined my reputation by saying that Creffield had seduced me". Maud Creffield, who was with her husband when he was shot, took strychnine while being detained in jail under a murder indictment for participating in the killing of Mitchell. Esther Mitchell was found not guilty by reason of insanity and committed to the Washington State Insane Asylum for three years. She was paroled April 5, 1909 and returned to Waldport, Oregon. She married James Berry in April 1914 and died August 1, 1914 of a self administered dose of strychnine. She is interred in Fernridge Cemetery, Waldport. Berry then married her sister Donna Mitchell Star and later Molly Hurt, all former members of the Holy Roller Creffield sect.

"Several of the women in Creffield's group of followers were confined to the Oregon Insane Asylum by family members. Use of the commitment process by family members was typical of the times." Oregonian July 13, 1906

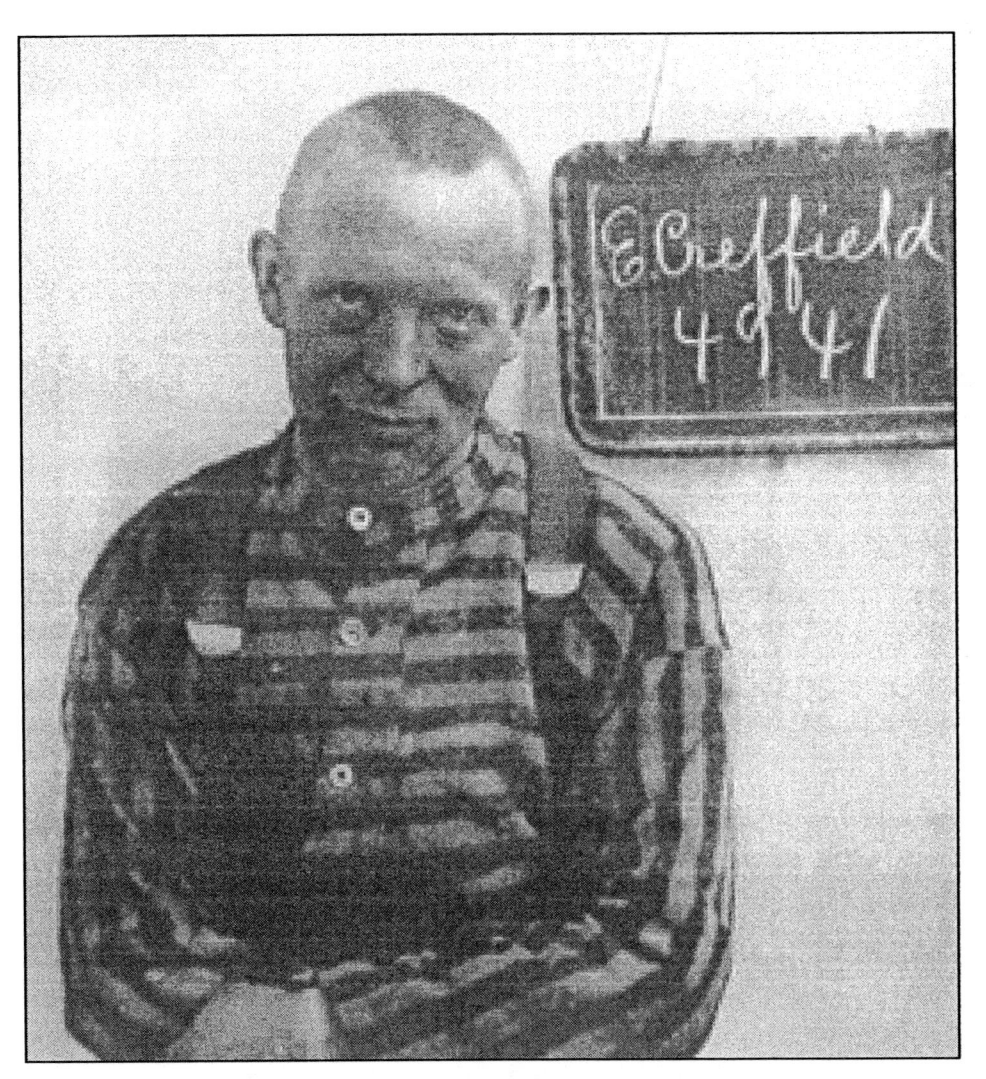

Franz Edmund Creffield Inmate 4941 was convicted of adultery and incarcerated at OSP September 16, 1904 with a two year sentence but was released 15 months later
Photo OSP

Frank Hamilton Curtis
May 7, 1912 - September 30, 1912

Frank Hamilton Curtis was born on May 23, 1868 in Matoon, Illinois to Thomas Curtis and Lucinda M. Hamilton, and emigrated to Oregon by way of Missouri. He married Lillian in 1896 and they lived in Portland. He was the assistant superintendent in 1912 when his boss, Charles W. James, Superintendent fell out of favor with Governor Oswald West.

West proposed a cost saving measure of firing the Superintendent (James) and continuing the Assistant (Curtis). Curtis would be expected to perform the duties of the Superintendent while being paid as the Assistant Superintendent. West also fired the chaplains as well as Curtis wife Lillian who served as a matron to women prisoners.

August 8, 1912, The Capitol Journal newspaper reported the manufacture of counterfeited half dollar coins in the penitentiary. Coins were moulded in the prison machine shop and passed in a local store by a trusty convict. This activity had been in progress for three weeks when discovered.[31]

Curtis was an interim superintendent serving until Governor West could appoint Berton K. Lawson. Curtis was a loyal employee who served the state well. He and his wife and family moved to Portland, where he served as Chief Deputy Sheriff in the Criminal Division of the Multnomah County Sheriff's office.

Curtis was the first president of the Grain Handlers Union in Portland and was a member of the Masonic and Elks lodges in Salem. His last employment in Portland occurred at the Swan Island Ship Yards. Curtis died October 26, 1943 at Good Samaritan Hospital in Portland. He was 74. He and his wife were the parents of five children; Thomas, Irene (Rice), George, Frank and Charles Curtis

Photo OSP

Curtis grave marker in the Rose City Cemetery in Portland.
Photo: Sue Woodford

Average number of inmates: 437
Number of employees: 40 [32]
Number of Escapes: None

Berton K. Lawson
October 1, 1912 to March 8, 1915

Berton K. Lawson was born April 11, 1876 to Foster Lawson and Emma Johnston in Chicago, Ill. He was appointed by Governor West to carry out the Governor's policies on prison reform (such as use of the honor system). The Governor dismissed veteran superintendent James over the honor issue and on an interim basis asked warden Franklin Hamilton Curtis to assume responsibilities held by James. Curtis was replaced by Lt. Colonel Lawson who had a strong military background.

The Capital News November 20, 1912, reported "the first work that will come under his hand will be the grim task of officiating at the execution of Jack Roberts, Mike Morgan, Frank Garrison, Noble Faulder, John Taylor and possibly the Humphrey boys on Friday, December 13, 1912." The first four were executed the same day and the Humphrey boys, George and Charles were executed March 22, 1913. Politically, Lawson opposed capital punishment.

Photo Portland Police Museum

During his career Lawson was credited with several prison reforms, notably use of the honor system, and the banning of stripped uniforms for convicts. The wardens report of October 4, 1914 stated, "Oregon State Penitentiary was known as a hard prison, with stripped uniforms, shaving the head, the dungeon, whipping post and hosing all in use."[33]

In 1914 Lawson was sent by Governor West to establish martial law in Copperfield, Oregon near Baker City. The town was in the hands of a gambling gang and the Baker County Sheriff and city officials refused to clean it up. The governor's secretary Fern Hobbs, was sent by train to Copperfield (with Lawson and several guards) to show that, "even a woman with law and order on her side," could make them knuckle under. Lawson is credited with the cleanup.

Lawson recommended that OSP be allowed to build four new moderately priced cottages for officers and their families. He estimated that two thousand dollars each would cover the cost of the cottages. He stated, "As it is now several of our officers live downtown and are not available in emergencies. A deduction of $10.00 per month could be made for rent of these cottages."

In 1913 women inmates were moved into the front part of the prison building. Lawson reported, "these quarters are better equipped, containing bedrooms, dining room, living room, bath, etc. They are provided with bed linen, their food is plain, wholesome and sufficient. Their exercises and recreation are adequate. They are taken for a long walk every morning, weather permitting." " Their occupation is cleaning and repairing books for the Oregon State Library, but as this work is not steady they are unemployed a good deal of the time except for their own fancywork." "They are allowed to write one letter a week."

In 1914 voters in Oregon repealed the death penalty.

Lawson was married to Jordan Belle Lilly and had one son B.K. Lawson, Jr. He was called to active duty in World War I. He served at Ft. Stevens where he was commanding officer. He was a Lieutenant Colonel at the time of his separation. He had also served in the Spanish American War. He was active in public affairs in Southern Oregon, Cottage Grove and Portland. He worked on the successful campaign of Joseph K. Carson for the position of Mayor of Portland. In 1933 he was appointed Chief of Police for the City of Portland by Carson.

He died February 27, 1948 in the Veterans Hospital. He was 71. He is interred in the Veterans Circle at Riverview Cemetery in Portland.

Number of employees (September 30, 1914): 38
Number of inmates: 413
Escapes: 52[34]

Lawson's grave marker at Riverview Cemetery in Portland.
Photo Sue Woodford

1910 Inmate Baseball Team called "House Team"
Photo OSP

Harry Percy Minto
March 23, 1915 – September 27, 1915.

Harry Percy Minto was born October 16, 1864 to John Minto and Martha Ann Morrison Minto. He was raised on the family farm in south Salem. He was married to Jessie Glenn. Harry Minto had served as City Marshall of Salem from 1892 to 1896. He was employed as Shop guard at the prison in 1895-96, and Sheriff of Marion County for two terms leaving that office in 1910.

Harry was appointed Superintendent of the Oregon State Penitentiary on March 23, 1915 by Governor Withycombe. He was killed in the line of duty just six months later on September 27, 1915.

Events leading up to the death of Superintendent Minto reported in the September 28, 1915 Lebanon Criterion Newspaper are as follows; "He was killed instantly at 11:30 p.m., September 27, 1915 as the result of a gunshot wound to the head."

The shooting occurred on the Albany Salem road two miles north of Albany. Superintendent Minto and a party were trailing Otto Hooker, the escapee and had been notified that he had shot Jefferson City Marshall J J. Benson and was headed toward Albany.

Otto Hooker was described as a physically fit inmate with a low level of intelligence. He was easily led by more aggressive inmates.

Photo OSP

Killed in the line of duty

A party including Minto, Walt Johnson of Albany, Sam Burkhart, penitentiary guard, left Albany in an auto and had proceeded along the road when they suddenly ran onto the convict. In an exchange of shots, Minto was killed. None of the other men in the posse was injured.

Otto Hooker eluded capture for one day when late the next evening a telephone call was received by the sheriff advising that Hooker had been located under a house in East Albany. The house was surrounded. After the man was ordered out of his place of hiding he made a move as if to draw his gun and was shot by policeman J. L. Long, inflicting a fatal wound. Inmate Otto Hooker was serving an indeterminate sentence from Umatilla County for the crime of burglary. The Daily Oregon Statesman Newspaper of September 30, 1915 reports "Hundreds Honor Slain Official." "The body of Harry Minto laid in state in the home lodge of the Salem Elks. Funeral services were held at 10 a.m. and at 11:20 the body was sent to Portland for services by the Portland Elks Lodge and later cremation." Prominent citizens of Salem offered eulogies in honor of Minto's dedicated service.[35]

Crematory records reflect that his ashes were provided to his nephew Doug Minto. Harry Minto is thought to be interred in the Minto family plot in Salem Pioneer Cemetery. His wife Jesse Glenn Minto is buried in Cox Cemetery founded by her maternal grandfather Thomas Cox, owner of Salem's first grocery store.

Number of employees: 38[36]
Number of inmates: 373
Escapes: 2

A home on Saginaw Street in Salem, formerly owned and occupied by the Minto family. Photo: Sue Woodford

A home on Saginaw Street in Salem, formerly owned and occupied by the Minto family. Photo: Sue Woodford

John W. Minto
September 28, 1915 – November 27, 1916

John Wilson Minto was born September 27, 1848 in Salem, Oregon to John Minto and Martha Morrison Minto.

John was appointed Superintendent in the wake of his brother Superintendent Harry P. Minto's death. John had applied for the superintendent's job at the same time Harry did. Harry was appointed and John went on with his business. John had previously served as Salem City Marshal in 1880. In 1891 he worked in Portland as a U.S. Weigher and Gauger. In 1910 he was listed in the census records as a contractor in Portland. John was well connected in both Salem and Portland communities.

Minto grieved the loss of his brother at the hands of an escaped convict and let it be known that escapees would be dealt with severely. Towards that end he reinstituted harsh punishment as discipline for rule infractions.

Publicly he advocated the segregation of prisoners in order to protect the young and accidental criminals from those who were criminals by choice. He reported that first offenders should be protected from the evil influences of repeat offenders.

Photo courtesy Oregon State Library

In spite of the work programs developed by John Minto the success of his tenure as superintendent was questioned by a committee appointed by the governor. A report of 1917 by L.T. Wentworth, E.E. Brodie and F.W. Mulkey found, "the conditions behind the prison walls to be deplorable." The disciplinary reports of the day reveal hosing, whipping, chaining to the cell door. Minto restored use of the bullring requiring convicts to walk in a circle without stopping daylight to dark. Those sent to the bullring area were celled in open air cells in all weather conditions. After the report was presented to the governor, John Minto's resignation was requested, November 14, 1916.

John Minto introduced the first sizeable flax industry inmate work program at the prison. From that time on it expanded from year to year to become the prisons leading industry. The best years for sales occurred in 1944 and 1945. Later when newer fibers were developed the flax industry was abandoned.

Minto was married twice. His first wife was Rebecca H. Yocum. His second wife Kate Sullivan. With Kate he had a daughter Laura Minto.

John Minto died August 30, 1926 at his home on Sunnyside Road in Clackamas County. He was the owner of Te-A-Wha Nursery. He was 77. He is interred in the Portland Memorial, Portland.

Number of employees (9/30/1916): 40
Number of inmates: 509
Escape and not returns: 22[37]

MINTO ASKED TO RESIGN AS PRISON HEAD

Action by Board of Control This Morning Is Direct Result of "Hosing" of Convicts Last Week.

SHERIFF ESCH MAY BE GIVEN THE BERTH

Governor Withycombe Makes Investigation and Finds Punishment Cruel.

Salem, Or., Nov. 14—The state board of control, consisting of Governor Withycombe, State Treasurer Kay and Secretary of State Olcott, voted unanimously this morning to demand the resignation of Warden John Minto as head of the Oregon prison.

The board decided to meet again in a few days and name his successor.

The dismissal of the warden is a direct result of the hosing of Jeff Baldwin and James Curtis, two convicts, on Sunday, November 5. The revival of the barbarous custom brought a storm of criticism from over the state and Minto was allowed to tell his story.

Monday Governor Withycombe investigated the facts on his own account and laid the facts before State Treasurer Kay and Secretary of State Olcott today. The result was the vote that will end Minto's career as warden.

Sheriff William Esch, of Marion county, is mentioned as a possible successor of Minto's.

When informed by telephone of the board's action Minto said his resignation would be filed right away.

Governor Sees for Self.

When Warden Minto was brought before the board last week and questioned in regard to the affair he made light of it and maintained that it was nothing more than a "wetting down," which was more than deserved by the unruly prisoners involved.

"To determine matters to my own satisfaction and get absolutely first hand information I went to the penitentiary yesterday and interviewed Deputy Warden Sherwood, the four guards who participated in the hosing, the two convicts who were hosed and two other convicts who witnessed at least some of the proceedings."

Oregonian Newspaper Nov. 14, 1916

WARDEN JOHN MINTO, whose resignation as warden of the state prison is asked, because of his policies.

Minto was asked to resign as a result of "hosing" of convicts.

Cremains and marker at the Portland Memorial for John Minto.
Photo Sue Woodford

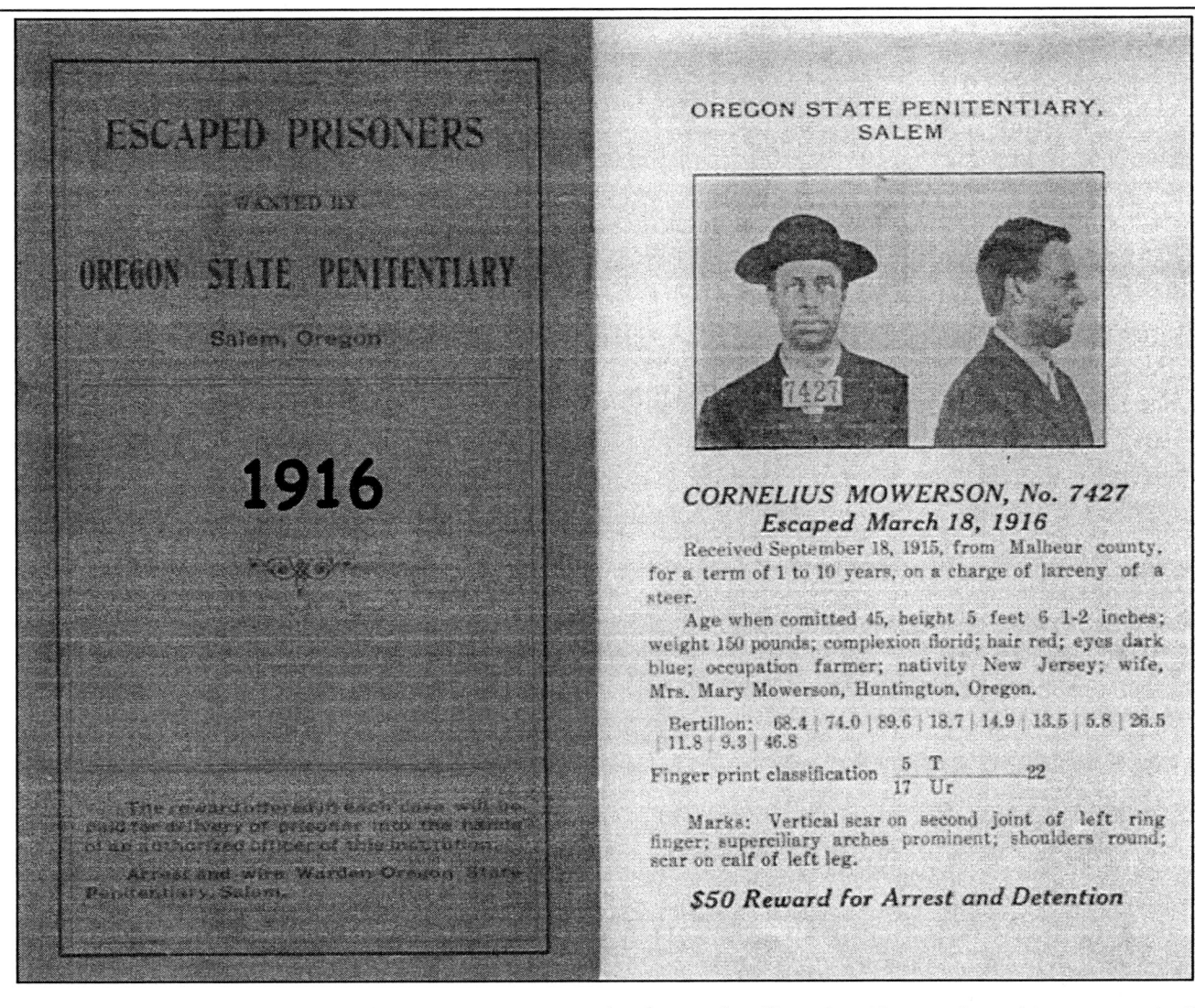

Escaped Prisoners Booklet: issued by Joe Murray, OSP chief records officer. Booklets such as this were periodically issued to inform the public — and bounty hunters — of escaped convicts and potential rewards.

Three tower on the newly constructed brick wall. The Oregon State Hospital is visible in the background

Charles A. Murphy
November 27, 1916 to December 3, 1918

Charles A. Murphy was born in Salem, on June 15, 1868 to William P. Murphy and Sarah E. Murphy. During the Spanish American War he served with the famous second Oregon Regiment in the Philippine Islands, was commissioned an officer in that organization. When Eastern Oregon State Hospital was under construction at Pendleton, Captain Murphy was superintendent of construction. At the completion of the institution he remained as engineer for the plant. He was called by Governor Withycombe to become Superintendent of the Oregon State Penitentiary.

Superintendent Murphy abolished use of the bullring as a disciplinary measure and introduced kitchen duty such as peeling potatoes for rule infractions.

Murphy's reform policies were short lived because of the occurrence of 58 escapes during the span of 1917 and 1918.[38]

Murphy established a lime plant at Gold Hill where inmate workers were employed. He also had inmates working on a wood cutting project which furnished fire wood for the Oregon State Hospital.

The flax mill employed the major portion of inmates at all times. Reported earnings of the inmates employed in the flax industry for a two year period was $9,426.07.

Murphy believed in providing elementary education to inmates and devoted a corner of the inmate dining room for that purpose. The school area was outfitted with slates, text books and writing tablets. He indicated that the foreign born inmates especially benefitted from learning to read and write.

Photo courtesy Oregon State Library

Murphy's other improvements include: planting flower gardens in the enclosed grounds, installing better lighting on the outer walls, establishing a trusty honor lodge called a mutual welfare league for inmates which meets weekly to resolve problems, housing one man per cell, allowing inmates to raise and lower the American flag daily in the yard.

After leaving the state prison office he entered the building industry and supervised the building of the Eastern Star Home at Hillsboro. He was Building Inspector of the Portland City School system, later serving as Federal Building Inspector in Portland until his retirement.

Murphy was married to Flora M. Simmons. He died January 2, 1945 at 76. He was survived by three sisters; Mrs. Emma Murphy Brown, Salem, Mrs. J. H. Robnett, Albany, Mrs. H. L. Lamourex, Seattle, Washington He is interred in the Pioneer Cemetery in Salem.

Number of employees (9/30/1918): 45
Number of inmates: 310
Highest number of inmates (3/8/1916): 566
Number of escapes 1916 22, 1917 30, 1918 28[39]

Murphy abolished use of the bullring as a disciplinary measure and introduced kitchen duty such as peeling potatoes for rule infractions.

He believed in providing elementary education to inmates and devoted a corner of the inmate dining room for that purpose.

Murphy's Grave marker at Pioneer Cemetery Salem. Photo: Sue Woodford

Samuel C. Worrell, standing. Worrell was employed at OSP as a guard. He is wearing the uniform of the day and a circular badge with a star in the center. Truck driver and passenger's names are not known. 1916
Photo: Sergeant Tom Burke

OSP Walls with towers one, nine and eight as seen from Mill creek This postcard is postmarked 1910

Robert L. Stevens
December 3, 1918 to May 30, 1919

Robert L. Stevens was born February 8, 1866 in Westfield, Hampden Co., Mass. He immigrated to Oregon in 1883. He graduated from the University of Oregon Law School in 1904. He then went to New York where took post graduate work in Banking and Finance at Columbia University.

Stevens served three terms as Multnomah County Sheriff from 1906 to 1912. He was a respected community leader in Portland at the time of his appointment to the position of Superintendent of the Oregon State Penitentiary by Governor Withycombe. He served only 6 months in the position.

In a report of the Oregon state board of control, "Trouble at the state penitentiary culminating in serious riots among the prisoners early in 1919 led to the resignation of superintendent Bob Stevens."

During his six months in office he strongly advocated greater cooperation in policing functions between City, County and State Police agencies. For seventeen years he was in the banking business in Portland, associated with Ladd & Tilton Bank. A cousin who also immigrated to Oregon from Westfield, Mass, Theodore Burney Wilcox was initially affiliated with Ladd & Tilton as a bank clerk until offered the opportunity to manage Flour Mills on which William Ladd had issued foreclosure notices. Wilcox as known as a Captain of Industry and Magnate of the China Flour from 1884 until his death in 1918. Robert Stevens connections with highly regarded business men in Portland were an asset to him in the positions that he held in Public Service.

Photo OSP

Robert Stevens served as Superintendent of the Pacific Livestock Exposition in 1935. Stevens died December 29, 1936. He was 70. He was single and was survived by two cousins, Mrs. Theodore Burney Wilcox (Nellie Sarah), Portland, and Lt. Col. Edwin R. Van Deusen, Ft. Sill, Oklahoma. He is interred at the Portland Memorial in Portland.

Number of employees: 48
Number of inmates: 373
Number of escapes: 9[40]

"Trouble at the state penitentiary culminating in serious riots among the prisoners early in 1919 led to the resignation of superintendent Bob Stevens."

Cremains and marker at the Portland Memorial for Superintendent Robert L. Stevens
Photo: Sue Woodford

OSP Shoe Shop — All shoes worn by inmates were constructed in the shoe shop by inmate workers
Photo OSP

Robert E. Lee Steiner, MD
May 30, 1919 to February 1, 1920

Robert E. Lee Steiner was born September 26, 1869 in Bluffton, Allen County, Ohio. His parents were Gideon Steiner and Elizabeth Hass. He came to Salem in 1886 at the age of 17. He was employed as a drug clerk. His pharmaceutical work in Steiner's Drug Store led him to the medical profession. He graduated from Willamette University with an M.D. degree in 1897.

He practiced medicine in Dallas, later moving to Lakeview where he was elected to the state legislature. He represented Klamath, Lake, Crook and Wasco counties.

About 1908 Steiner was appointed by the governor as superintendent of the Oregon State Hospital. The hospital grounds encompassed 1,520 acres and in addition to the hospital facilities included orchards, a dairy, a truck garden, poultry house and silos. In 1913 a crematory was built on hospital grounds, later referred to as "Steiner's Chimney." It still stands today.

Photo courtesy Oregon State Library

"Governor Olcott prevailed upon Steiner to lend his administrative ability to straighten out a difficult situation. He served as superintendent of the penitentiary for the greater part of the year. He visited many of the state prisons in the country, and through the knowledge thus gained, coupled with his talent for managing difficult people, he so improved the penitentiary situation that he was able to return to his post at the hospital." Steiner returned to Oregon state hospital on February 1, 1920 having completed the necessary turn-a-round at OSP.

In 1913 a crematory was built on hospital grounds later referred to as "Steiner's Chimney."

Steiner supported the controversial sterilization legislation enacted in Oregon for certain inmates of OSH and OSP. In 1918 the State Board of Health ordered the sterilization of twenty persons. The Board approved 17 cases submitted by the Oregon State Hospital. Twelve of the 13 men were castrated and four women received ovariotomies according to the Oregon State Hospital Eugenics record.

In 1928 Steiner recommended a ward at the penitentiary be set aside for housing the criminally insane, removing them from the State Hospital

Dr. Steiner appeared to be closely allied with the Salem Clique. (An insider group of Oregon opinion-leaders). He was a respected member of the community and well connected politically. In 1892 Steiner married Belle Golden, of Salem. They had three children, Rita, wife of D.J. Fry, Jr. (Rita had two children; Daniel J. Fry, III

In 1920 voters in Oregon restored the death penalty.

and Marylee.), Barbara wife of Captain Earl C. Flegel (Barbara had one son, Earl C. Flegel, Jr.) and Milton B. Steiner, MD.

He died December 20, 1947 at the age of 78. He is interred in Mt. Crest Abbey Mausoleum, Salem.

Number of employees: 48
Number of Inmates: 373[41]

Steiner used pharmaceutical work in Steiner's Drug Store as a stepping stone to the medical profession. He is shown here playing chess with colleagues in Steiners Drug Store, Salem
Denton photo Salem Public Library Collection

The former Steiner home is located at 537 High Street in Salem, It was built in the 1920s and occupied after 1936 by Steiner and his wife. His daughter Rita married Dan Fry and lived across High Street.

Steiner's cremains and marker   Mt. Crest Abbey Mausoleum, Salem
Photos: Sue Woodford

OSP Receiving gate for trucks entering the prison 1934

Louis Hartt Compton
February 1, 1920 to May 1, 1922

Louis Compton was born November 16, 1883 in Odessa, Missouri to Anna Peyton and Gresham M. Compton. The family moved to Caldwell, Idaho in 1890 where Graham Compton had a homestead.

After completing schooling in Caldwell, Louis enlisted in the U.S. Army. He served twenty two months in the Philippine Islands returning to Idaho. He came to Salem as local Secretary for the Young Men's Christian Association. He held this position until 1916 when he was called to service as a First Lieutenant in the Third Oregon Infantry. He received numerous citations for his service in the military including the French Croix de Guerre. He was discharged and returned to Oregon and his work with the YMCA. Shortly thereafter he was appointed parole officer by Governor Olcott.

Photo courtesy Salem Family YMCA

Eight months later Compton took over the administration of OSP from Dr. Steiner. Steiner was held in high regard as the administrator of the Oregon State Hospital and held that position concurrent with his position at the prison. He worked with Louis Compton to develop policies that were later carried out by Compton. Compton credits Steiner for the substantial improvements made to OSP physical plant during Compton's administration.

The facility had fallen into disrepair when Steiner took over and he developed a maintenance and remodeling plan implemented by Compton. According to the annual report to the governor the old kitchen was a disgrace to the institution. The old execution room, just back of the dining room, was remodeled and the kitchen and bake shop were moved in there, an up-to-date electric bake oven installed taking the place of the old brick oven. The heating system in the cell house was very unsatisfactory in that the radiators were on the outside of the cells, keeping the corridors warm but radiating very little heat in the cells where it was needed This was supplanted by an individual coil in each cell.

Inmates enjoyed motion pictures as part of their recreation. Universal Film Exchange, Inc. of Portland furnished the prisoners films one night a week, gratis. T.G. Bligh and son Frank Bligh furnished the inmates a good show or two during the holidays [42]

Compton was married to Bertha V. Sharpe, March 21, 1910. They had one son, David R. Compton (Mary J. Crites). Louis H. Compton died March 20, 1952 in Los Angeles, California and is interred in the Los Angeles Veterans National Cemetery. Bertha V. Compton died July 18, 1964 in Portland

Employees as of September 30, 1920: 44
Inmates as of September 30, 1920: 268
Highest number of inmates: 566
Number of escapes: 27[43]

Comptons grave stone at Los Angeles Veterans National Cemetery Photo Sue Woodford

OSP ovens and inmate kitchen help with staff in background. Stoves built by inmates in the foundry. Photo OSP

Film Projection Room OSP Theater. Photo Jim Ramsey

Foundry buildings at Oregon State Penitentiary - early post card

James W. Lewis
May 1, 1922 – January 15, 1923

James W. Lewis was born March 21, 1868 in Corvallis, Oregon to John Harrison Lewis and Martha Ann Means. In 1910 James lived in Salem, and was employed as a bridge foreman for the Railroad. In 1920 he was working as a warden at the Penitentiary.

James "Big Jim" Lewis served as Superintendent of OSP under two appointments, the first in 1922 by Governor Ben W. Olcott, and the second in 1931. His 1922 appointment will be covered here and his 1931 appointment later in this book.

A number of improvements were added to the institution, The principal one being the addition of a cement flume which replaced the old wooden one. Other improvements include paving of the avenue leading from the streetcar line on State street to the front gate and from there to the State Hospital. Other work included paving of roadways inside the prison yard, construction of a cement sidewalk laid from the street car line to the main entrance and beyond to the garage. The construction of a modern green house; remodeling and repainting the dairy barn, horse barn and machinery shed all occurred during the Lewis administration.

Photo OSP

The main entrance to the yard was moved from the south side of number one tower to the north side. Lewis proposed the purchase of the 47 acres of land east of and adjacent to the penitentiary. The land, owned by heirs of the Savage family could not be purchased earlier because the heirs were unable to give a clear title to the land. George Savage at the September 30, 1922 date of the annual report was able to furnish a clear title.

James W. Lewis was married to Winifred Dayton Lewis. He died October 28, 1938 at age 70. He was serving in his second appointment as Superintendent of Oregon State Penitentiary at the time of his death. He resided on the penitentiary reservation at Route. 6, Box 1, Salem,. He is interred in City View Cemetery, Salem.

Employees as of September 30, 1922: 48
Inmates as of September 30, 1922: 453
Escapes: 8[44]

The main entrance to the yard was moved from the south side of number one tower to the north side.

Johnson S. Smith
January 15, 1923 – October 8, 1923

Johnson Smith had a varied background. He was born in Caldwell, Ohio February 7, 1866. He attended college in Ohio and taught school in Iowa, Kansas, Nebraska and Oregon. He served in the Oregon Legislature in 1896 representing Linn County.

He was in the newspaper business in Albany, Oregon in 1897 and 1898. He moved to Union County in 1898 and taught school in Union and Wallowa counties. He was appointed deputy warden at Oregon State Penitentiary July 1, 1903 a position he held until July 1, 1907.

He was Deputy Collector of Internal Revenue Service in 1913 and served also as chief deputy. He resigned to run for the third congressional district in 1918. He was not elected and continued his position as deputy collector in 1919. He was appointed first federal prohibition director, January, 1920. He held that office until 1921 when a change of administration occurred. In Oregon prohibition became law in 1916 before the 18th amendment was adopted nationally.

Oregon Magazine 1923

He was appointed Superintendent of OSP January 15, 1923. Superintendent Smith was a humanitarian who espoused a "soft glove" approach in the handling of inmates. He voiced the opinion that good health, skill, education and attitude were critical to an inmates success when they returned to society as free persons. He believed that inmates ought to be reformed in prison by the use of humanitarian prison management methods. He decried the brutality of previous administrations.

His lenient policy is blamed for 37 escapes in his first 6 months as superintendent. Three inmates had multiple escapes.

Three weeks before his dismissal the most disastrous fire in the history of the prison to that date, occurred entailing a loss of $151,029.52. The fire swept through all the penitentiary shops. Insurance on the stored Flax lost in the fire, was $40,000. The Emergency Board appropriated an additional $65,000 to rebuild the shops. The reconstruction was accomplished for $60,000 and $5,000 was returned to the Emergency Board in 1925 by Smith's successor Dalrymple.

Smith struggled to preserve his power in light of a well planned political move to discredit him and mold public opinion against his humanitarian efforts. A former newspaperman, Smith outlined his policies in an article in the Oregon Magazine after he had been dismissed from his position as Superintendent of OSP. Johnson further stated, "The greatest curse of prison management is the stool pigeon system. There have been times in the Oregon State Penitentiary that the institution was run by an illiterate guard and a group of degraded and often degenerate inmates. These stool pigeons were ready to destroy their fellow inmates for their own advancement and the guards and officers who used the stool pigeon system were ready to take their word unsupported. I know cases in the past where men were placed in solitary confinement for years on the word of a stool pigeon without heat or light except what could come through the grated door, with very meager food supply and no reading matter of any kind. No prisoner should ever be allowed to even discuss his fellow prisoner with a guard or an officer in a derogatory manner, on the other hand no officer or guard should ever make a pet of one prisoner and persecute another. Next to the stool pigeon system, the enforced idleness of prisoners is the most damnable thing that these unfortunates have to endure."

He later moved to Portland where he served as State Deputy Insurance Commissioner. Johnson Smith and his wife Esther had two sons; Robert W. Smith, and Asa C. Smith. Smith died January 29, 1938, Portland.

Note: A subsequent effort by A.M. Dalrymple to obtain funding for fire protection at the penitentiary was turned down by the Emergency Board.

Statistics for the items below are covered in the biennial report of A.M. Dalrymple
Number of Employees September 30, 1923: 48
Number of Inmates September 30, 1923: 443
Number of escapes: 38[45]

"Next to the stool pigeon system, the enforced idleness of prisoners is the most damnable thing that these unfortunates have to endure."

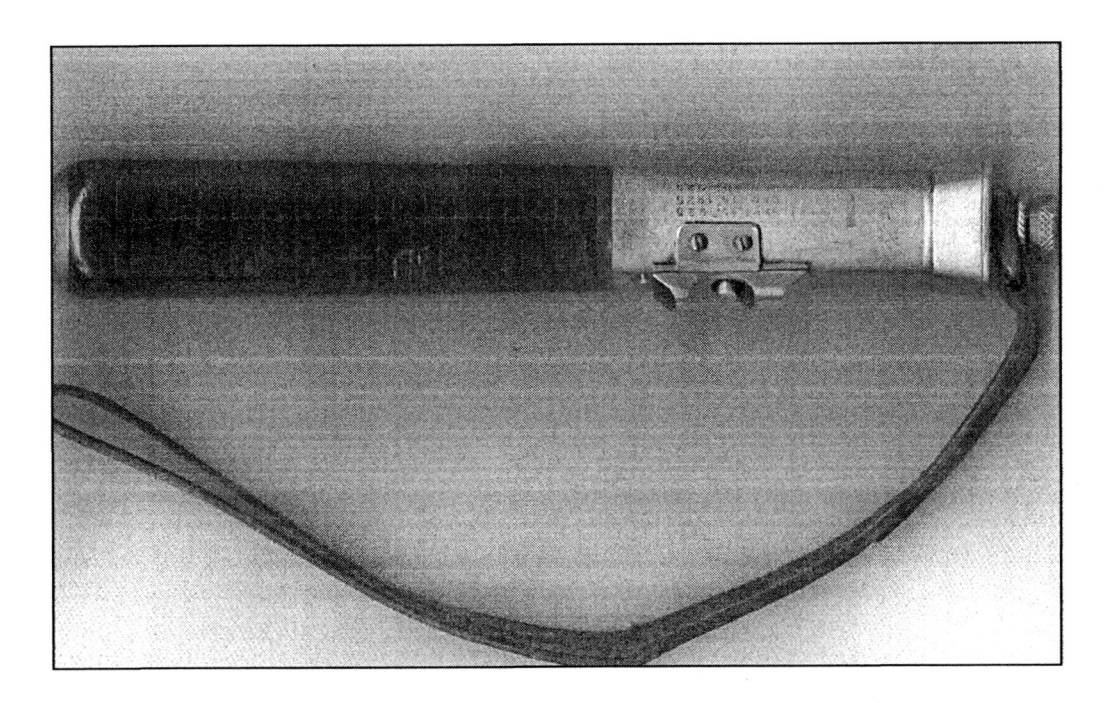

A 1929 Federal gas billy. Billys were used in riot control at OSP. The handle of the billy unscrewed and a tear gas charge was loaded. The charge could be fired and the billy used in its conventional manner as a club.

Amos M. Dalrymple
October 8, 1923 - December 5, 1925

Amos M. Dalrymple was born in Elkhorn, Walworth County, Wisconsin in 1867. He was the son of Hamilton Sherman Dalrymple and Sylvia Johns. He migrated to Oregon and married Adelaide Holman daughter of Margaret and Hardy Holman of Polk County. They had a son Denton F. Dalrymple. In 1900 Amos Dalrymple was employed as a printer. He was working at OSP in the commissary by 1910 and was a faithful employee through the years.

Highlights of Amos Dalrymple's administration include installation of an electric light plant at OSP using a powerful water wheel. This electric plant furnished 65% of the institution's electricity. The prison suffered a major fire three weeks before Dalrymple was appointed, recovery from the financial loss was slow. Dalrymple was able to construct an inmate recreation room in the recreation yard. This was a major benefit as before this time inmates were confined to their cells during inclement weather. Dalrymple recommended the "colony plan" which consisted of "a good farm of 300 – 400 acres separate and away from the main building, where the younger and better class of prisoner and those with short terms might be kept by themselves."

Photo Oregon State Library

The escape of four desperate criminals occurred August 12, 1925 resulting in the death of guards J.M. Holman, and John Sweeney, as well as Bert "Oregon" Jones, a convicted desperado. Holman was Dalrymple's brother in law, having been on the job just two weeks at the time of his death. Governor Walter M. Pierce appointed a special committee to investigate the conditions inside the prison leading to the escape. The Committee returned it's report to the Governor while Superintendent Dalrymple was out of state attending a five week

Dalrymple's brother in law was a guard at the prison. He was killed in the line of duty during a prison escape Aug. 12, 1925

Amos Dalrymple relaxing on the front lawn of the prison. OSP Photo

Power generation plant at Oregon State Penitentiary. Dalrymple installed the hydroelectric plant at the prison during his tenure It generated all the power needed for the prison operation..

conference of prison officials at Jackson, Mississippi, and inspecting a large number of penal institutions in the Eastern United States. The report of the Governor's committee was made public December 6, 1925.[46]

Amos Dalrymple worked as a US District Court Bailiff in Portland after he left OSP. He died April 4, 1945 at St. Vincent's Hospital in Portland at the age of 71. He was survived by his wife Adelaide. He is buried in Dallas City Cemetery, 2065 SW Fairview Ave., Dallas, Oregon.

Number of employees as of September 30, 1924: 49
Number of inmates: 416

Amos Dalrymple grave marker at Dallas City Cemetery, Dallas, Oregon
Photo: Sue Woodford

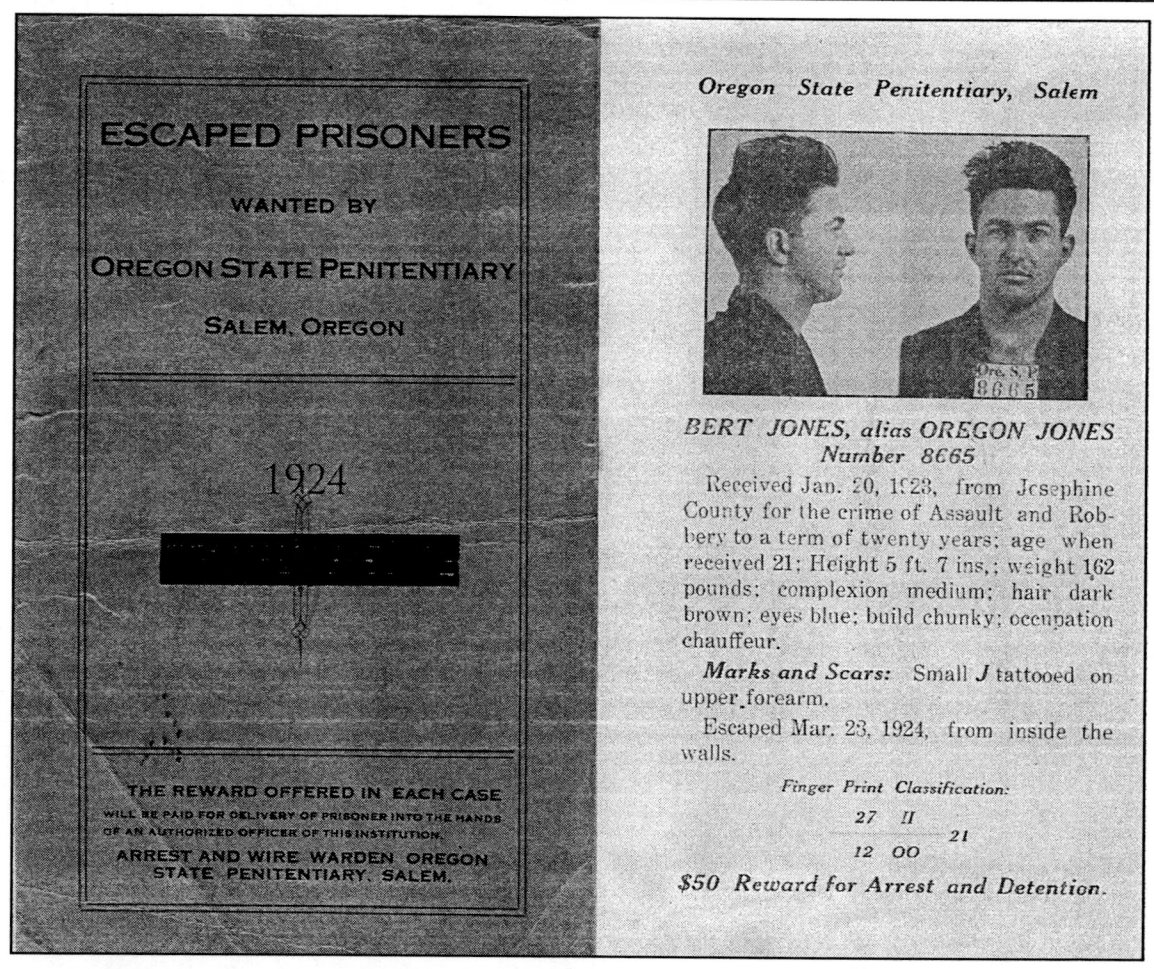

Escaped Prisoners Booklet - issued by Joe Murray, OSP chief records officer. Oregon Jones was one of the prisoners that later escaped in August, 1925. Guards J.M. Holman and John Sweeny were killed during the escape..

Famous Oregon outlaws: The DeAutremont brothers robbed a Southern Pacific train October 11, 1923 were convicted of murder and train robbery in Oregon in 1927, sentenced to life in Oregon State Penitentiary. Hugh paroled 1958, Ray paroled 1961, Roy died in the state hospital years after a pre frontal lobotomy.
Gravestone at Belcrest Cemetery, Salem Photo: Sue Woodford

John William "Will" Lillie
December 5, 1925 – April 1, 1927

Will Lillie, was born January 23, 1886 to Charles and Josephine Llewellyn Russell Lillie at the family ranch near Mayville, one of four brothers. He received his advanced education at McMinnville College (later Linfield College) and Portland Business College.

He was married in 1907 to Ethel Goff. They became homesteaders in the Buckhorn area of Gilliam County. Sons Elton and Byron were born in 1908 and 1912.

Lillie successfully ran for the office of sheriff of Gilliam County in 1914. At 27 years of age he was the states' youngest sheriff. In 1923 he accepted the appointment by governor Pierce to the position of deputy warden and later superintendent of the Oregon state prison, at Salem. He was known as a strict disciplinarian at a time of considerable prison turmoil. When Amos Dalrymple left the position of superintendent there was a report generated calling attention to the lack of training and discipline among the guards when an escape occurred. Also, a focus of the report, was the ages of the guards who were in their 60s. It was recommended by the investigators that," no man should be employed as a wall guard who is not between the ages of 25 and 50 years old."

Lillie believed in providing a "distinctive uniforms for all guards"

In a press release after Lillie's appointment he reported that, "politics hereafter will be eliminated in the selection of employees at the Oregon State Penitentiary and every guard will be compelled to have certain qualifications satisfactory to the prison officials."

He indicated he would, "employ guards between the ages of 25 and 30 years of age who must be physically fit." He proposed installation of a huge siren to sound as a warning to persons living several miles in either direction of the prison. The siren was to be used only in event of a prison break or some other serious disturbance involving the convicts.[48]

Adoption of distinctive uniforms for all guards was proposed. Superintendent Lillie planned to segregate trustee inmates employed outside the walls of the prison to stop the smuggling of contraband into the prison. Improvements completed at the prison by Lillie included the erection of a new tower outside the main gate of the prison, removal of the prison arsenal from the turnkeys' office in the administration building to the new tower, elimination of the "dog house" within the institution enclosure, and installation of barbed wire barriers on the top of the walls. The "dog house" was a slang term for the segregation unit where troublesome prisoners were housed. He left the prison in 1927, upon the change of governors.

After leaving OSP, Will Lillie served for a time as business manager of Hot Lake Sanatorium near LaGrande, and later as a Multnomah county welfare investigator, at Portland. Near the conclusion of WW II, the family purchased a farm near Hillsboro. Will died suddenly at the Hillsboro farm May 3, 1947, and is interred in Lincoln Memorial Park, Portland. He was 61.

Number of employees: 60
Number of inmates: 547
Highest number of inmates (7/31/26): 592
Number of escapes: 26[49]

Will Lillie grave marker at Lincoln Memorial Park, Portland. Photo: Sue Woodford

OSP Superintendent's office during Lillie's term as Superintendent. Photo: OSP

Henry W. Meyers
April 1, 1927 to May 1, 1931

Henry Meyers was born June 2, 1869 in Glenville, Kern County, California, the son of Ellen Harvey and Joseph Meyers. The family came to Salem, January 20, 1880. Joseph purchased the White Corner General Store. Henry attended Willamette University. He and his brother Milton purchased their father's business in 1906 and operated the store for fourteen years under the name H.W and M. L. Meyers. In 1920 the store was bought by Miller Mercantile Co. Henry Meyers was Secretary and Manager of the Miles Linen Mill.

He was appointed as Superintendent of the Oregon State Penitentiary April 1, 1927 by the State Board of Control during Governor Patterson's administration. He devoted most of his time to developing the Industries Program at the Penitentiary. Meyers made substantial improvements and changes in light of severe overcrowding at the penitentiary. Changes included installation of a fireproof vault, construction of a vegetable root storage house and installation of ornamental double steel gates to the avenue leading to the prison. Construction of a new guard tower midway between the towers number 4 and 6 occurred. A complete concrete fish ladder and fish rack was built with plans approved by the Game Commission. An overall cleaning and repainting of walls, corridors, doors, ceilings to main cell blocks, commissary and all other departments occurred.

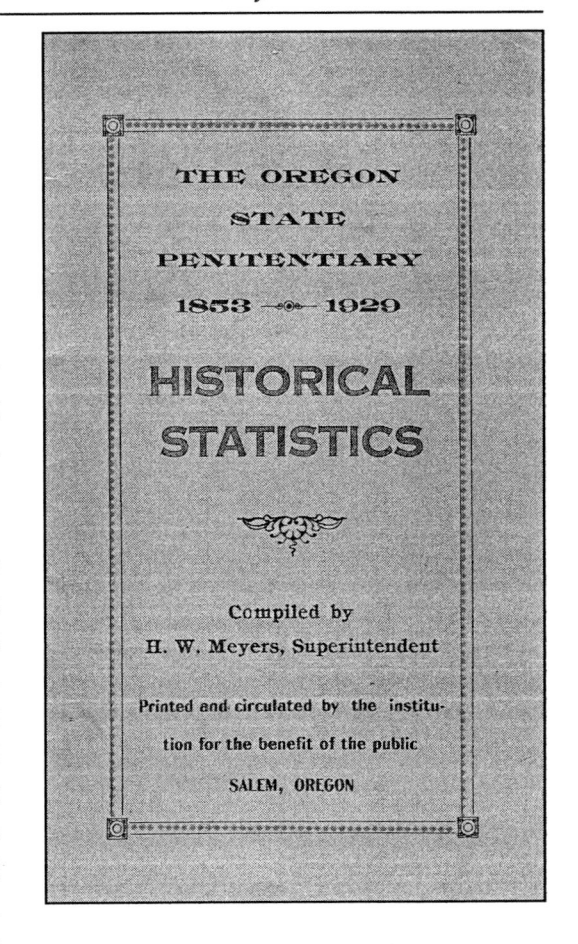

The biennial report describes the overcrowding as very dangerous, "with 112 inmates being tucked away where ever there might be room for a bed, very much like a country hotel when there are 25 percent more guests than the accommodations were ever intended for." The boys' training school (504 acres) was turned over to the Oregon State Penitentiary when the boys' school was moved to Woodburn in March 1928.

In 1929 Henry Meyers compiled a book titled, *"The Oregon State Penitentiary 1858-1920 Historical Statistics printed for the benefit of the public."* A section of that booklet devoted to flax development states, "This (OSP) flax plant is the most complete and largest of any in the entire world." The booklet also states, "For many years the federal government had no prison for its female prisoners and the Oregon State Penitentiary was selected to care for those convicted in Oregon as well as adjacent states, the United States Government paying therefore, the sum of $40.00 for each woman thus confined".[50]

Meyers left the position of superintendent during an apparent political squabble between Governor Meier and members of the State Board of Control. Governor Meier, claiming a mandate of the people, warranted his assumption of total control of the Oregon State Penitentiary and ten other state institutions from the Board of Control. Meier called for the dismissal of Superintendent Meyers. He did not prevail when State Treasurer Thomas B. Kay and Secretary of State Hal E. Hoss voted against the proposal. Even though Superintendent Meyers had the support of Hoss and Kay, he decided to resign.

"This flax plant is the most complete and largest of any in the entire world"

In 1896 Henry Meyers was married to Ellen Eades Meyers daughter of Rhoda Chapman and George A. Eades. George Eades was a former sheriff and county clerk of Marion county. Meyers was a member of the Benevolent and Protective Order of Elks and a supporter of efforts to build the Salem General Hospital. During WW I he was active in the American Red Cross serving as director of the Willamette chapter. He died March 24, 1939 at his home at 430 N. Summer Street in Salem. He is interred in the Pioneer Cemetery. We have been unable to locate a photo of Henry W. Meyers.

Number of employees as of September 30, 1930: 75
Number of inmates as of September 30, 1930: 915
Number of escapes: 3[51]

Henry Meyers grave marker at Pioneer Cemetery, Salem   Photo: Sue Woodford

Flax Operation OSP file

OSP Administration Building 1920s. OSP file

Old postcard of OSP prison cells A block

By action of the Legislature in March 1929 the former Boy's State Training School was turned over to the Oregon State Penitentiary. Shortly thereafter a fire occurred pictured here. The building was renovated at a cost of $35,000 and housed 50 trusty prisoners in 1930. The facility was then known as the Farm Annex

OSP women inmates sewing uniforms. Initially women were housed at the State Training School, later moved to OSP

James W. Lewis
October 1, 1931 to October 28, 1938

James W. Lewis served two terms as Superintendent of OSP, the first in 1922 (May 1, 1922 to January 15, 1923), the second term October 1, 1931 to October 28, 1938 when he died in office.

Lewis was popular with the inmates. When Superintendent Meyers appointment was under review by the governor the inmates were reported to be shouting, "give us Lewis".

While Lewis was superintendent inmates were provided with a library and allowed to bring books to their cells, they had an orchestra, recreation such as boxing matches and baseball games. The prison had a full time dentist as well as a full time physician and Lewis recommended provision for a full time educational director.

The University of Oregon provided correspondence courses to all prisoners desiring to avail themselves of such courses. A request was made for an intercommunication telephone system to connect all departments and the guard towers. This telephone system was installed. Lewis recommended repeal of the indeterminate sentence law and in it's place provide determinate sentences thereby allowing for good time credits to be earned. This law change would allow inmates the opportunity for parole when certain conditions had been met. The law was passed by the legislature.

Photo OSP

Lewis implemented the installation of a cafeteria dining system in the inmate dining room. Inmates could take all the food they wanted but were required to eat all they took. Lewis also recommended that guards who in years past had been required to work every day including Sundays, be allowed to receive at least one day off each week. This request was granted and in addition guards were provided with two weeks vacation with pay each year.

When Lewis died while in office it came as a shock to his colleagues in state government. Lewis was highly regarded by state officials. Governor Charles H. Martin said; "I always have found warden Lewis sound, sensible and familiar with prison discipline. He was firm but just and free from that misdirected emotionalism which at times wrecks such institutions. It is going to be a difficult task to find a warden so thoroughly equipped by character and training to succeed him"[52].

State Treasurer Holman described Lewis as "a splendid gentleman and an honest and courageous warden. Lewis was at all times a square shooter with the convicts and they respected him. I considered Lewis my personal friend." Secretary of State Snell: "Jim Lewis was not only one of the best wardens Oregon has ever had but he was outstanding in such service in the entire United States. He had the unusual faculty of gaining the admiration and respect and absolute confidence of the prison inmates. His word was as good as his bond. Oregon has suffered a serious loss. "It is noted that the Prison Farm Annex taken over by OSP in 1929, provided vegetables, dairy products, meat from hogs, poultry and cattle, as well as most of the eggs consumed by the inmates. In 1936 a cottage was constructed at a cost of $4,000 on the prison reservation. This was the home occupied by the superintendent.

Jim Lewis passed away at his residence at OSP (Rt 6, Salem, OR) October 28, 1938. He was 70 . He was married to Winifred Dayton Lewis. He is interred at the City View Cemetery, Salem Honorary pallbearers at his funeral included Governor Martin, Secretary of State Snell, State Treasurer Rufus Holman, Willamette University President Bruce Baxter, State Police Superintendent Charles Pray. A bronze plaque honoring Superintendent Lewis was installed in the prison

Number of employees 1932: 75
Number of inmates 1932: 846
Escapes: 8[53]
Number of employees 1936: 71
Number of inmates 1936: 987
Number of escapes 1936: 9
Number of employees 1938: 73
Number of inmates 1938: 1095
Escapes: 3[54]

Lewis recommended that guards who in years past had been required to work every day including Sundays, be allowed to receive at least one day off each week

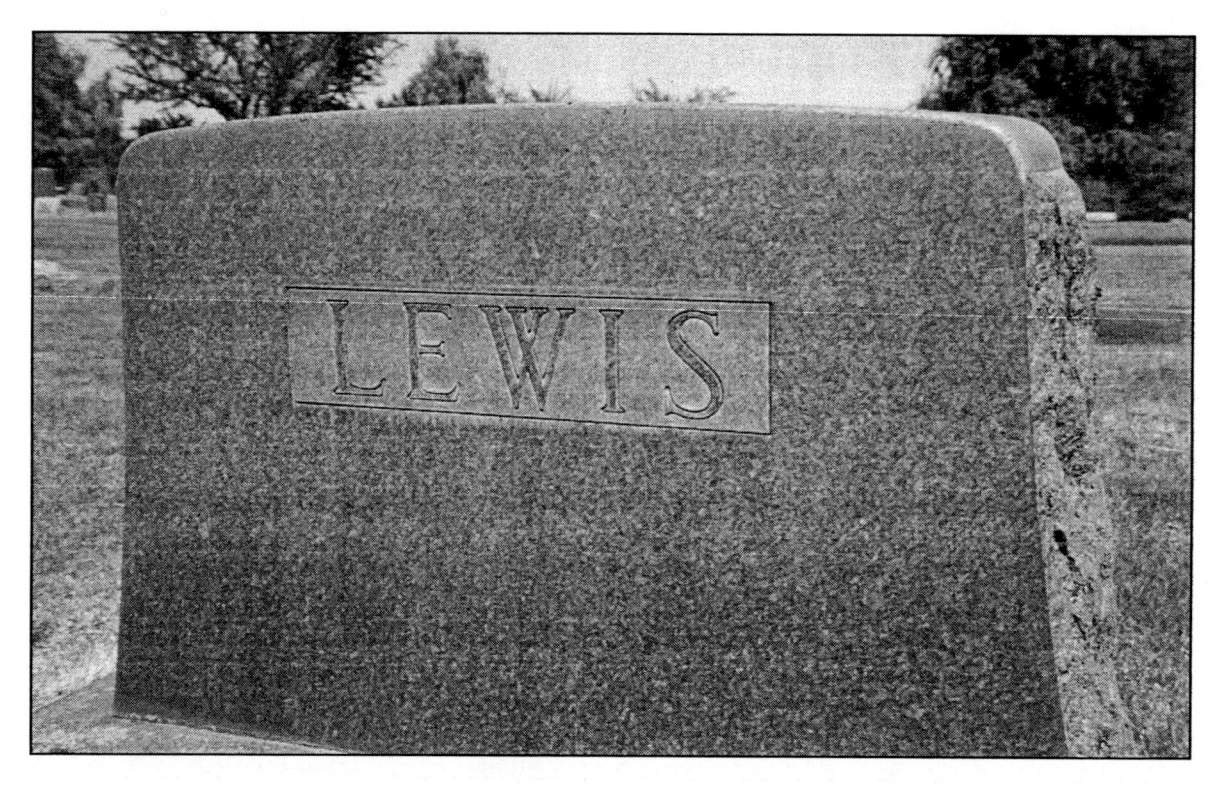

Jim Lewis grave marker is located in City View Cemetery, Salem.
Photo: Sue Woodford

Receiving Gate OSP 1935 Later designated as an historical landmark. Photo OSP

The Riot of 1936

July 31, 1936, as a result of the Oregon state court taking away the ability for inmates to earn and be credited with "good time" towards the completion of their sentences, inmates at the Oregon State Penitentiary rioted. Cell blocks were damaged, the butcher shop was torn apart and equipment strewn about. The commissary and adjacent storage room were looted and goods boxed up to be carried out as contraband.

Cleaning up after the riot of 1936. Photo OSP

January 31, 1937, Salem experienced one of the heaviest snow falls in history. A record 27 inches of snow fell in an 18 hour period. The Prison Farm Annex and Tuberculosis Hospital lost electricity. Portland General Electric workers on skis were sent to find the break in the line. Top photo Oregon State Penitentiary front entrance facing State Street, photo below is taken from the doorway shown above. Photo OSP

Chief Records Clerk

From 1911 to 1953, Joe S. Murray served as chief clerk of the Oregon State Penitentiary records office and was in charge of the Bertillion records. He also maintained the fingerprint bureau of the Oregon State Police, which was located within the prison. An early corrections history reports Murray as one of the leading experts of criminology on the Pacific Coast. He was born December 8, 1882 and died March 6, 1980.
Stephen A. Stone, Oregon Memorabilia, 1967 Parkstone Co. with permission

Joe S. Murray

Badge courtesy Sergeant Tom Burke

Birth of the Oregon State Police

Law enforcement and the apprehension and incarceration of convicted felons changed in the 1930s and 1940s. The senate passed the bill creating the Oregon State Police Department on February 25, 1931, and the house approved it on March 1, 1931. An announcement was made March 24, 1931, that the new department would begin operations on August l, 1931 Captain George C. Alexander was placed in charge of the Bureau of Identification and Investigation at general headquarters and charged with the investigational activities of the department. He was appointed deputy superintendent January l, 1932, and served in that capacity until his appointment as superintendent of the state penitentiary on December l, 1938. Fingerprinting and identification cards were maintained at the Oregon State Penitentiary until July 1941, when they were transferred to state police general headquarters in the state capitol.

82 *Oregon State Prison Superintendents - The Shepherds of State Street*

Badge Oldest OSP Guard's Badge. Photo: Jim Ramsey

Badge, Early OSP Officers Badge. Photo: Jim Ramsey

Oregon state prison guard uniform buttons and hat buttons, owned by officer Ruggles. Photo: Sue Woodford

George Cassie Alexander
December 15, 1938 – April 1953

George Alexander was born January 11, 1885 in Hillsboro, Oregon. He was married to Faye Corwin August 11, 1912. George C. Alexander was appointed superintendent of Oregon State Penitentiary, resigning his position as deputy superintendent of the Oregon State Police, December 15, 1938. He replaced James W. "Square Deal Jim" Lewis who died while serving as superintendent. At the time of his appointment the institution had 73 employees and 1095 inmates. The superintendent's title was changed to warden

The principal industry at the penitentiary was the flax plant. This program was started in 1915 for two major purposes, to furnish labor by the prison inmates and to foster an industry for the state which could not be pioneered without public support. Alexander initiated construction of a new dining room with a capacity of 1200 inmates in 1940. He recommended that the state furnish uniforms for the guards. Up to that point employees were required to purchase their own uniforms and Alexander proposed that uniforms be made in the prison tailor shop at a small cost. He felt the administration would be in a better position to demand that they always be kept cleaned and pressed.[55]

Photo: OSP

He recommended license plates and road signs be manufactured inside the walls to help employ more inmates. These programs were projected to employ 30 to 50 inmates. Inmate idleness was a problem. In 1942 the number of staff was 82 and the number of inmates 909. There were 18 escapes in 1942. Three executions took place in the prison gas chamber.[56]

By June 30, 1944 the number of employees was 78 and number of inmates 830. (Decline of the inmate population is attributed to young men enlisting in the military service). There were 33 escapes and two executions in the gas chamber. Two years later the number of employees climbed to 87 and inmates to 1037. There were 48 escapes and five executions in the gas chamber.[57,58]

By 1948 the number of employees was up to 99 and inmates 1255 with two executions and 28 escapes. A fruit and vegetable cannery was constructed on penitentiary grounds, paid for by funds from the Prison Revolving Fund. Modern cannery equipment was installed and the canned products were used in state institutions.

He recommended license plates and road signs be manufactured inside the walls

After a six day sit down strike by inmates a recommendation was made to move Alexander out of the warden's position into a newly created superintendent's position and to appoint Virgil O'Malley to replace Alexander. The two served in tandem until O'Malley was fired in April 1953 and Alexander retired at the same time.

George C. Alexander died October 29, 1972. He was preceded in death by his wife Faye Corwin Alexander, November 19, 1968 and a daughter Katherine in 1925. They are interred in the Pioneer Cemetery in Hillsboro. Alexander's had three children; Dorothy Stadter (wife of Marion County District Judge Edward O. Stadter Jr.), Charlotte Wendel and son George C. Alexander Jr.

George Alexander's grave marker at Pioneer Cemetery Hillsboro.
Photo: Sue Woodford

Pre-World War II Inmates on the recreation yard enjoying July 4, 1941 celebration
Photo: OSP

Virgil J. O'Malley
September 1951 to April 1953

Virgil James O'Malley was born March 26, 1903 in Pioneer, Cedar County, Iowa, to Peter J. O'Malley and Nancy E. Hempy. He moved from Iowa to Vallejo, California, where he was a student at Mare Island Naval Hospital.

He was employed later as associate warden of California State Prison at Soledad.

Virgil O'Malley's tenure with OSP was short and somewhat troubled. He was appointed in September 1951. At the time of his appointment he talked at length about the classification system he had in mind to set up training on, for staff. Unfortunately he appeared unable to implement it in the three months that lapsed between his appointment and a major escape attempt.[60]

On November 4, 1951, inmate John Pinson and nine others attempted an escape. They were within 50 feet of freedom when Guard Maurice Folquet foiled the escape attempt. December 1951, Guard Francis L. McConnell secretly brought in dynamite, a revolver and ammunition to inmate "Buck" Dupree Poe. They were turned in by another inmate.[61]

Photo OSP

On February 8, 1952 inmate Lawson David Shirk Butler escaped and was placed on the FBI "Most Wanted" list, later recaptured, April 21, 1953. During November 1953, inmates in the segregation unit ambushed and held five guards hostage.[62]

A blue ribbon committee of three wardens from Illinois, South Dakota and Idaho were invited from the American Warden's Association to do a study and fact finding of the Oregon State Penitentiary operation. As a result of this study the wardens recommended:
1) Hiring of a competent warden to take over immediately,
2) That all inmates be locked in cells and fed there until control and discipline can be restored,
3) That the Board of Control should set forth general policies and then turn full authority of the institution over to the warden (at this time George Alexander served as superintendent with O'Malley acting as warden. This split authority created operational problems.) As a result of the recommendations of the committee, Superintendent Alexander retired and O'Malley was terminated.[63]

Virgil J. O'Malley and his wife had two children, Patricia and Terrance O'Malley. Virgil O'Malley died January 13, 1986 in Sonoma, California..

Gas Chamber moved to second floor of Prison in 1938. It was brought to the prison on a railroad flat car in December 1937 installed February 7, 1938.
Photo OSP

OREGON STATE PENITENTIARY
GEO. ALEXANDER, SUPERINTENDENT
V. J. O'MALLEY, WARDEN

SALEM, OREGON
Jan. 2, 1953

MR. _____

THIS IS AN INVITATION FOR YOU TO WITNESS

THE EXECUTION ACCORDING TO LAW OF

Morris Leland and Frank Oliver Payne

FRIDAY, THE 9TH DAY OF JANUARY, 1953

BEGINNING AT 12:15 A. M. IN THE OREGON STATE PENITENTIARY

_____
SUPERINTENDENT

NOT TRANSFERABLE — PRESENT THIS CARD FOR ADMITTANCE

Morris Leland for the murder of Thelma Taylor, 15-year old high school girl at Portland, Ore., Aug. 6th, 1949, and Frank O. Payne for the murder of H. Nathan Butler, Portland grocer, Jan. 9, 1951, in a robbery attempt.

Clarence Theron Gladden
April 1953 – March 1968.

C.T. Gladden was born July 12, 1894 in Napa, California He was the oldest child of Isaac and Emma T. Gladden. His father, Isaac, was employed as a psychiatric aide in a California asylum.

During WW I Gladden was employed as a ship fitter on Mare Island Navy Yard. He was married to Margaret they had one son George Gladden.

Gladden started prison work in California then worked 23 years in federal prisons including Leavenworth, Kansas; Tucson, Arizona; Terre Haute, Indiana, and McNeil Island, Washington. He was assistant warden at McNeil Island Penitentiary when he was appointed to the position at OSP. News accounts indicate that he was offered the job because a riot was anticipated. When it came about three months after his arrival he put it down without loss of life and came out of it saying it had enabled him to do five years of work in four days. He launched new programs of rehabilitation and discipline. Oregon State Correctional Institution (OSCI) was completed in 1957 to house youthful offenders and remove them from OSP. A new cell house "A" block was completed in May 1957. A new boiler house located outside the walls completed September 1, 1958. Industries included: furniture factory, metal shop, laundry, mattress and upholstery shop, garage, and garment factory which manufactured inmate clothing and staff uniforms.

Photo OSP

The Oregon Women's Corrections Center (OWCC) was completed in 1964 with capability of housing 84 women inmates. This facility was constructed on the grounds of OSP, using inmate (male) labor. The women were moved from the women's ward inside the OSP administration building to the newly constructed women's center. The OSP Superintendent was responsible for OWCC until 1972.

In 1965 the Board of Control created a position of director of corrections to assist the Board of Control in supervising the institutions. This division of authority and unfunded program mandates led to unrest that erupted into the riot of March 9, 1968. The director of corrections, George Washington Randall, an unqualified person used a fraudulent resume to obtain the position. His deception was uncovered by the Marion County Grand Jury when he failed to follow basic corrections procedures during the riot. One of Randall's early unfunded debacles forced upon Gladden, was the Upward Bound educational program, directed by Thomas Gaddis with collusion from his associate, Ace Hayes. This program gave selected inmates preferential treatment, proliferated contraband within the institution, created animosity between educational staff, security employees and the Gaddis - Hayes duo. Gaddis and Hayes circumvented security procedures entering and exiting OSP. Gaddis, author of *The Birdman of Alcatraz* died October 10, 1984 in Portland. Ace Hayes died February 13, 1998. Gladden served 15 years as Oregon penitentiary superintendent when the riot occurred. He had been ill with cancer at his home about six weeks. The night of the riot the Board of Control announced the superintendent was to have announced his retirement in a few days. He was replaced by Hoyt Cupp whom Gladden had been training for the job.

Clarence Gladden died two months later in May 1968, at his newly constructed retirement home in Tacoma, Washington. He was 73. His wife Margaret died in 1989. They had one son, George Gladden. Clarence and Margaret Gladden are interred at the New Tacoma Cemetery, Tacoma, Washington.

June 30, 1954 Employees: 297[64]
Inmates: 1597
Annex: 150-175 Inmates, Forestry Camp: 60 Inmates Women's Ward (located on 2nd & 3rd floors of the Administrative Building) 28 Inmates
June 30, 1958, Employees: 305[65]
Inmates: 1512
June 30, 1964, Employees: 304[66]
Inmates: 1726

Clarence Gladden grave marker at the New Tacoma Cemetery
Photo: Sue Woodford

First Aid Training Class. Lt. Don Johnson is shown on far right in white shirt. Other officers are wearing the single breasted uniform jackets with epaulets on the shoulders and brass buttons Photo: Don Johnson

First Director of Corrections

In 1965 George Washington Randall, an unqualified person using a fraudulent resume was appointed to the position of director of corrections. His deception was uncovered by the Marion County Grand Jury when he failed to follow basic corrections procedures during the riot. Randall returned to North Carolina where March 28, 1972 he was appointed Secretary of Social Rehabilitation and Control. He died December 2, 1972 in an automobile accident.

"In summary, Mr Randall, is a 57 year old, who for the first 45 years of his life had no education, training, experience or apparent interest in corrections". "Because of his lack of training and experience he did all the wrong things [during the riot].

He has lost all respect in every agency involved in or with corrections."

George W. Randall Photo OSP

"George Washington Randall is completely unqualified and should be immediately removed as Director of Corrections for Oregon."
Page 20, Marion County Grand Jury report 1968[67]

Records Office OSP 1960s- This office housed all inmate records. Mrs. Burkett sitting at desk, Richard Smith kneeling looking at file. Records clerks (standing) updated files daily.
Photo: Ed Ben

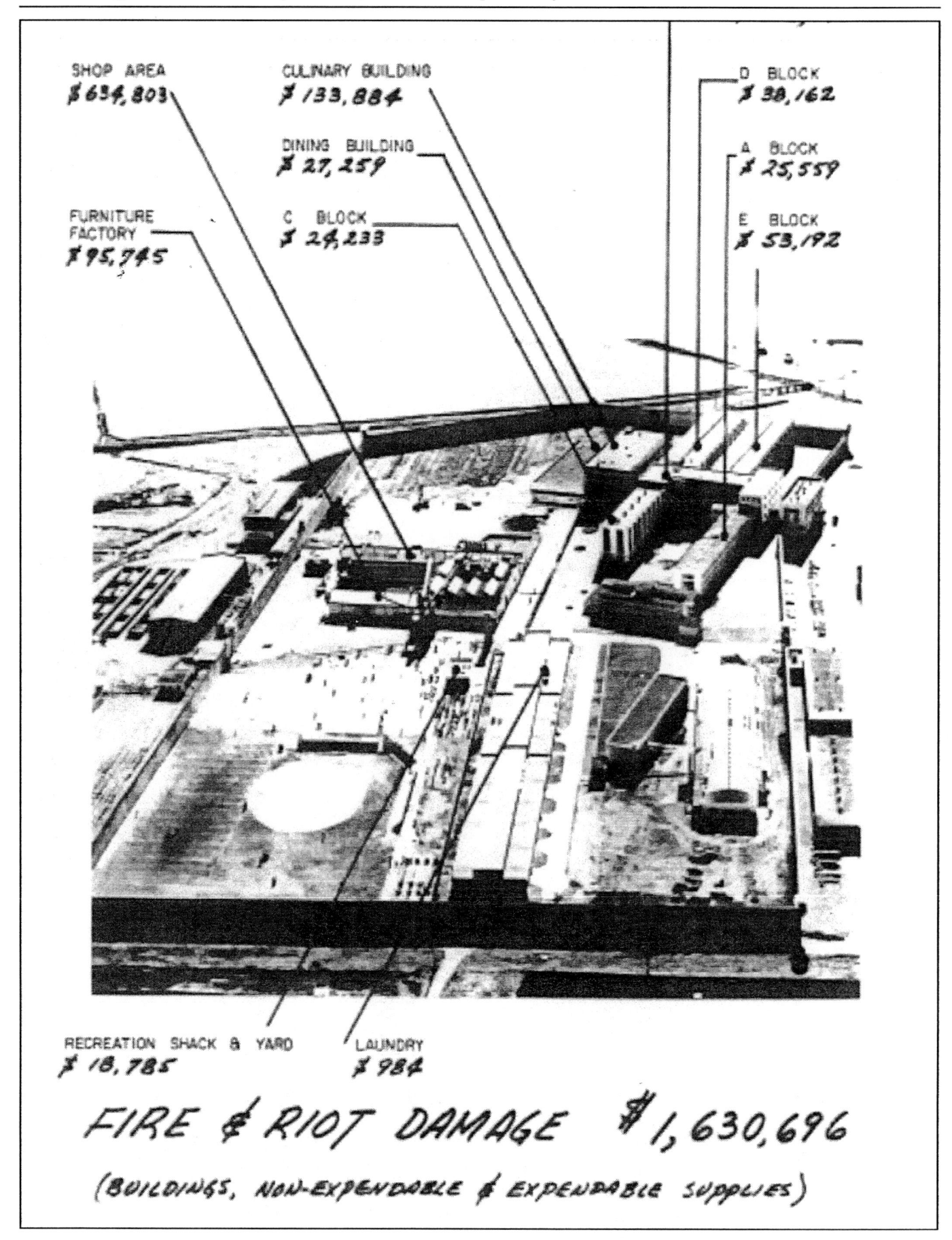

Estimated costs of fire and riot damage was $1,630,696.

Ed Ben looking through the 9x12 inch opening in the barred window through which he sawed his way out. He was trapped with inmates in the Hobby Shop on the Library floor during the riot. He was one of the many correctional staff who's lives were jeopardized by George Randall's incompetence.
Photo Ed Ben

Handcuffs and key

Guards Quarters OSP photo taken in 1934
Initially guards were required to live in these quarters if they were unmarried. Married guards could live at home or in the quarters. Later guards had the option of living on the reservation or elsewhere. Other state provided quarters included a dormitory located near the Dome Building. It was known as "Heartbreak Hotel" because many single or divorced officers lived there. Another dormitory was located at the Tuberculosis Sanitarian on Deer Park drive near the Prison Farm Annex. Photo: Jim Ramsey

OSP Prison Officers Baseball team
Back row: Ed Sparks, Ted Peterson, Harol Whitley, ?, Ed Ben, ?,? Ed Good
Front row: Don Johnson, Robert Geer, Bob Patton, Don Versteeg, Cole, ?
Photo: OSP

Guards Quarters Dining room circa 1953 Staff Meal tickets cost .35 cents a piece.
Photos Jim Ramsey

Inmates working in the furniture factory.
Photo: OSP

94 *Oregon State Prison Superintendents - The Shepherds of State Street*

OSP Chapel Built
The chapel was built by inmates in 1963. It was designed by Mockford and Rudd Architectural firm of Oregon City who periodically checked on the progress of construction by inmate builders. Lumber was donated by Georgia Pacific, Bohemia Lumber Company and Jones Plywood and Veneer Company. A rotating altar provides accommodations to Catholic and Protestant chaplains. Pictured here is Father Raymond Fritter, celebrating mass for Catholic inmates. OSP Photo: Grant Yoder

"Rule 11 Duties of Convicts: During Divine Service all convicts must sit erect during the delivery of the sermon; no lounging or hanging down of heads will be permitted. During singing and prayers they will assume such positions as are usual in the church of the officiating minister; provided the same is made known to them, otherwise a respectful and reverential position must be assumed. William Watkinds, Superintendent Biennial Report 1870"

Arsenal Corporal Rund 1960
Photo: OSP

Old wall is on left and new wall on right - new wall completed in 1950s.
Photo OSP

Inmate editor of inmate magazine Shadows.
Photo OSP

Badge: OSP Oldest Hat Badge
Photo: : Sergeant Tom Burke

Badge: Chapel Guard Badge of Don Johnson.
Photo: Harol Whitley

Badge: Assistant Captain of Yard Badge
Photo Jim Ramsey

Lieutenant Donald J. Johnson served as Chapel Guard early in his career with OSP. Photo: Maxine Johnson

Uniforms supplied by the prison

In 1940 Superintendent Alexander requested that the state purchase uniforms for the guards. He proposed that the uniforms be made in the prison tailor shop. Until that time guards were required to purchase their own uniforms which placed a hardship upon them. The first uniforms were gray. Over the years the style and color has changed. Hat badges were seen in photos taken in the 1940s. Uniform fabric patches were created and have undergone minor changes in recent years as the department has built new prisons rocker stripes were added above the department logo to designate the name of the prison in which the officer works

OSP hat badge, circa 1970

Southern Steel Cell House Key (reduced). Photo Tom Burke

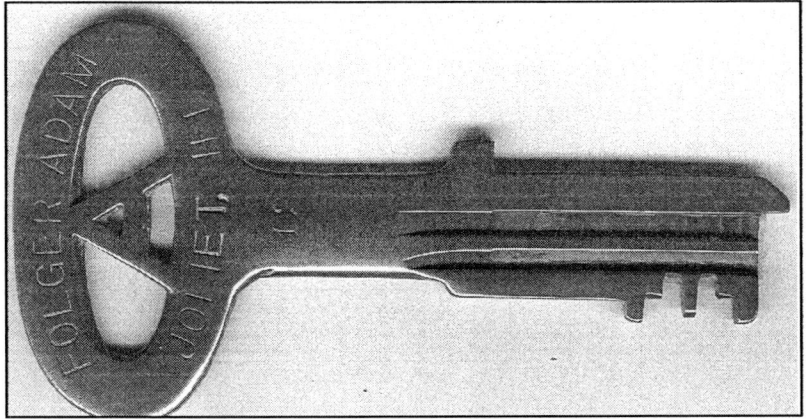

Folger Adams cell house key (reduced). Photo Tom Burke

Oregon State Penitentiary Pistol Team. Correctional staff once identified simply as "guards" achieved greater recognition for their professionalism when the civil service classification was changed to correctional officer. In the 1970s, gender bias was removed from the personnel rules, labor contracts and post orders providing a greater equality for women. Prior to 1972 posts were "manned," when women were hired they were "staffed." *Photo: OSP Archives*

Ed Ben with pistol competition trophy 1961. Ed is shown in the double breasted uniform with strips on the sleeves. *Photo Ed Ben*

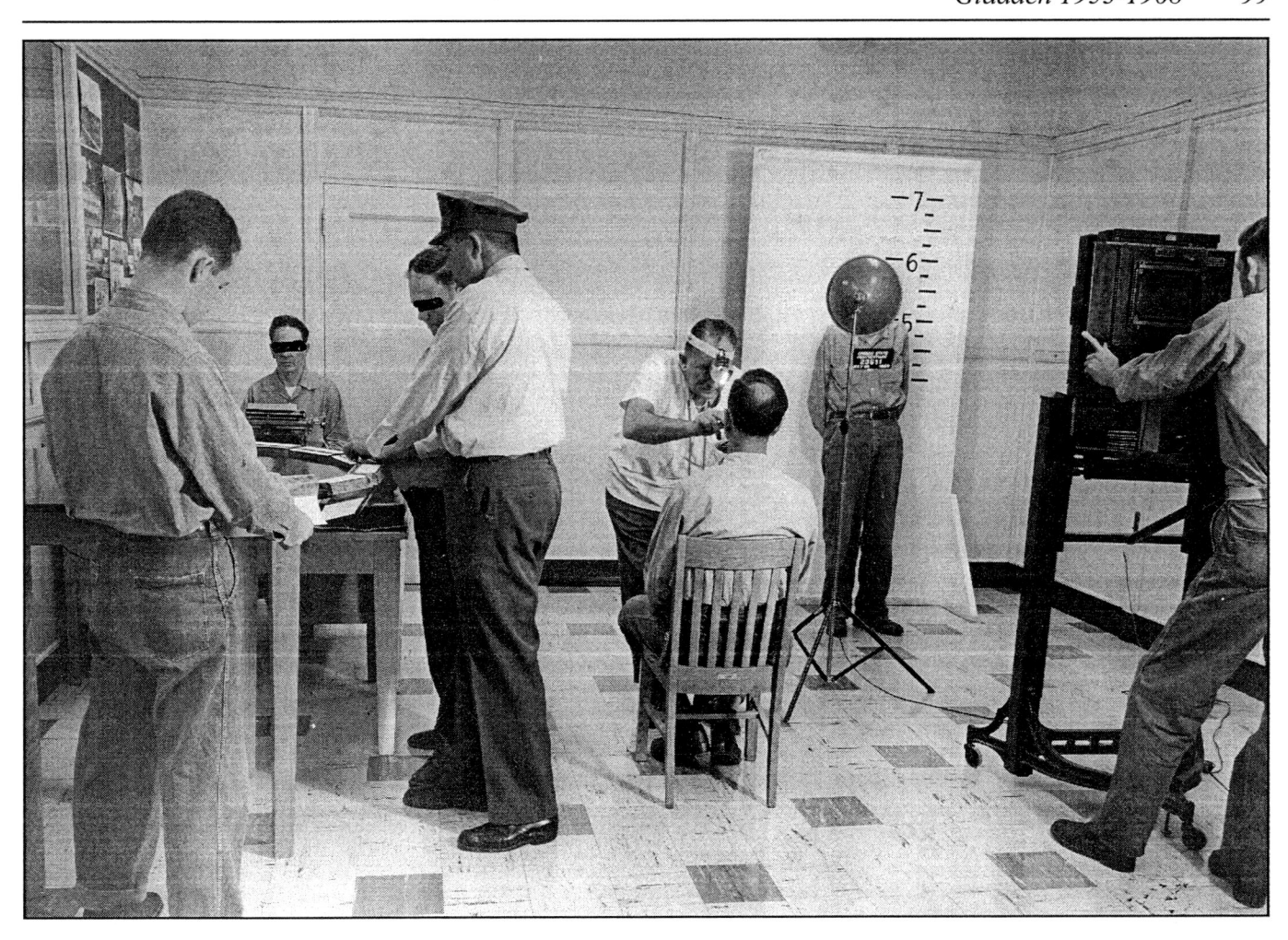

Officer Roy Amstutz, inmates and the prison dentist, Dr. Epeneter working together in the identification and intake process at Oregon State Penitentiary. Photo OSP circa 1967.

Classification System Established

In 1955, a Correctional Classification Board was created to establish a system of classification for persons committed to any correctional or reformatory institution. It supervised and controlled the transfer of inmates between institutions. Members were Chair of the State Board of Parole and Probation, Director of Parole and Probation, Superintendents of Oregon State Penitentiary, Oregon State Correctional Institution, and MacLaren School for Boys. In 1965, the Correctional Classification Board was abolished and its duties transferred to the newly created Corrections Division.

Inmates "walking the line"

Recall line from the recreation yard — inmates are moved from the recreation yard to the cell blocks or housing units. Inmates follow a red line painted on the avenue, guards can be seen on the left. During this daily process inmates would be randomly pulled from the line and "shook down" or searched for contraband. This photo was taken from 10 tower overlooking the yard. September 1954 Photo OSP

Far right: Hoyt Cupp, Harol Whitley and unknown officer on the rifle range. This station on the practice range was established at the same height as the towers on the OSP walls so guards could practice shooting accurately. OSP Photo taken 1954

These officers are shown in the uniform slacks, shirt and hat sans the double breasted jacket with striped trim on the sleeves. This grey uniform jacket was later change to a dark brown Eisenhower type zip front jacket with band around the bottom. Further changes in the uniform included a blazer type jacket with a cloth patch and in recent years an all weather jacket in black with grey shirt, black tie.

In 1964 Voters repealed the Death Penalty in Oregon. The Gas Chamber was subsequently removed from the Oregon State Penitentiary

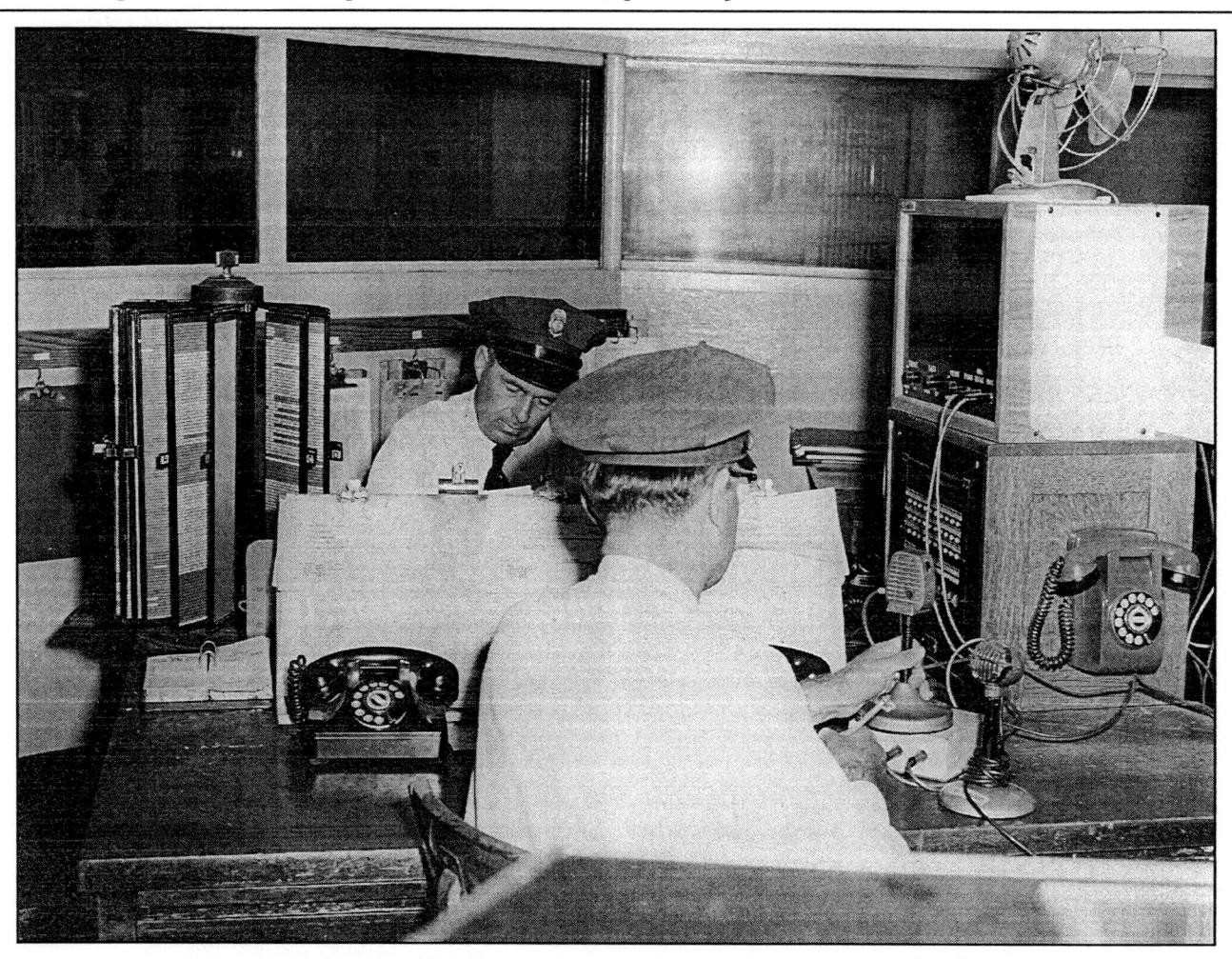

The Control Center staffed by officers Jack Roberts and Robert Wright. After the riot of 1968 the dial from the black telephone was salvaged from the wreckage.

Towers at OSP 1960s There are ten towers, eight towers located on the outer wall. Number one tower served as the arsenal and is located on the avenue leading to the prison. Number ten tower is a free standing tower in the center of the prison complex.

Hoyt Carl Cupp
March 9, 1968 – August 31, 1984

Hoyt Carl Cupp was born June 22, 1927, to Amanda Blanche Chase Cupp and Theodore Judd Cupp and raised in Salem.

His father died when Hoyt was 7 years old. He was raised by his mother. He graduated from Salem High School. He served in the U.S. Navy on the cruiser Springfield during WW II.

He went to work for the Oregon State Prison after returning from the service in 1948 at the age of 20. He worked in a variety of correctional officer positions working until 1953 when he was assigned to the position of training officer at OSP, a position he held for the next 6 years.

In 1959 he was promoted to the position of captain of security and was responsible for designing all security systems, developing policies and procedures and training all security staff prior to the opening of the newly constructed 450 bed Oregon State Correctional Institution.

Photo OSP

In 1967 he was appointed to the position of assistant superintendent at OSCI and was being groomed to take over the position of superintendent of OSP when the riot of 1968 erupted. At that time he was transferred to OSP and appointed superintendent. During the next years Cupp restored order to OSP and worked at developing a strong management team through whom he managed the daily operations at OSP. He regained the trust of other agencies which had been destroyed by Corrections Director Randall during the riot. Cupp served in the role of superintendent at OSP for 17 years.

He made daily trips inside, keeping an eye on all aspects of the operation. He was responsible for many institutional management innovations. He developed a full range of inmate recreational activities. He also converted OSP hospital to an infirmary dispensary convalescent ward and set up a system under which all major illnesses and injuries are treated by specialists in community facilities. He lobbied for a comprehensive vocational training program including in-house community college training for inmates. Under his direction OSP became a nationally recognized leader in developing systems of reasonable control of dangerous contraband and created a safe environment in which inmates and staff work together. He developed management teams to encourage a two-way flow of information and to tap considerable staff talent at OSP. He scheduled regular meetings with management teams formalized by recorded minutes.

Cupp enrolled at Western Oregon State College and over a period of 10 years obtained his Bachelors Degree in Corrections in 1977. He also graduated from the School of Correctional Administration at George Washington University.

He was married to Clara Cupp and they had two sons, Thomas and Benjamin Cupp, and one daughter, Cynthia Cupp. He later married Mary Caponette, they were divorced and he married Doris M. Haag in June 1984.

Hoyt Cupp died October 8, 1990 at the age of 63 in a hospital in Portland after a 19 year battle with cancer. Cupp was committed to serving the community, he was on the boards of the Salem YMCA, the Salvation Army, Camp Fire Girls and Salem Boys Club. He was past president of the American Cancer Society in Salem and was a member of the Quiet Birdman, a national pilots' organization. He was given a Paul Harris Fellow by the East Salem Rotary Club in 1990. He is buried beside his parents in the Pioneer Cemetery in Salem

During Cupp's administration the first female correctional counselors and correctional officers were hired. The first women appointed were Sandra Moore, Correctional Counselor and Debra Martin Dawes, Correctional Officer. Change did not come easy and at times required litigation to move forward.

One of Hoyt Cupp's strengths in managing the Oregon State Penitentiary was his excellent working relationship with the Oregon State Legislature. He was able to negotiate better salaries and benefits for employees. State Senators and Representatives were given tours of the prison and shared meals in the staff dining room. When Hoyt Cupp left OSP it was the end of an era where the superintendent was in charge of the prison. There after direction for operations of all prisons came from the director of corrections and a covey of administrative staff. Cupp initiated the unit team management system. He was acutely aware at all times of the safety and security of the institution. He regularly visited the yard as well as the cell blocks. He assured that the buildings were kept clean and freshly painted. The Farm Annex grounds were well kept with the fences being continually maintained in good order. The dairy herd won prizes at the Oregon State Fair.

Two cemeteries are located on the grounds of the prison farm. One belonging to the Herren family on who's homestead the farm is located, and the Boy's Training School Cemetery. Both of these cemeteries were well kept during Cupp's tenure as superintendent of OSP.

Number of employees: 496
Number of inmates: 1,500 OSP
                    200 Farm Annex
                      98 Forest Camp
                1,798 total

Cupps grave marker at Pioneer Cemetery Salem
Photo: Sue Woodford

1983 OSP Policy Staff
Front row: L. Kahle, H.C. Cupp, M. Weber, D. Karn, S. Hill, F. Bernt, R. Martin, B. Eckrode, C. Beals. Second row: T. Crowley, C. Keaton, J.C. Keeney, B. Chappelle, L. Roach, W. Bowles, Chaplain J. Jacobson, R. Hart, H. Whitley, C. Williams, W. Everetts, S. Gassner, G. Smetana, B. Schuck, S. Coleman, G. Morton, J. Seidler, D. Schumacher, M. Goraum, D. Spangrud, R. Seed, R. Inman, N. Armenakis; Back row: Chaplain M. Henry, C. Felker.

Seated at desk,: Hoyt Cupp, back row from left: S. Gassner, J.C. Keeney, B. Schuck, S. Coleman, C. Keaton. Front Row : H. Whitley, C. Williams. Photo Grant Yoder

First Escape in 26 Years Occurred October 31, 1979

A creative and unusual escape from OSP occurred October 31, 1979. Delbert Fuston and Wayne Strickland concealed themselves in a couch in the prison upholstery shop where Fuston worked. The couch was placed on a flatbed truck which was then driven to a warehouse just outside the prison walls and unloaded with a forklift. The pair waited inside the couch until 4 p.m., when the warehouse with the truck inside was locked up. The convicts then cut themselves out of the couch, removed the hinges from the warehouse doors and drove away in the truck. It was not known how they obtained keys to the truck.

Corrections officers in a guard tower at the penitentiary gate sounded a whistle in an effort to stop the truck. Police were called as soon as the truck left the prison. Penitentiary employee, Norm Newberry saw the fleeing truck as he left work for the day and followed it in his own car.

According to police reports with Newberry in pursuit, Strickland and Fuston drove to the large Center Street NE complex which houses Salem Hospital General Unit, Oregon State Hospital and the offices of the state Corrections Division. There they encountered Debra Godwin, a Corrections Division records clerk, who was getting into her car on 23rd Street NE north of Center Street. "I had my keys in my hand, and one of the guys jumped out of the truck and forced me into my car," Godwin said. The other convict then got into the car, and each held a knife to Godwin, who sat between them on the front seat. They drove toward D Street. Newberry apparently witnessed this from his own car, according to the police report

"The one that was driving held a knife to my arm," Godwin said, and the other convict held a knife to her chest. She described the knives as "crude." "When they first got in they just said they wanted the car and told me to shut up," she said. Godwin said she told the men she is a divorcee with two children and "I explained to them that all the kids had was me. Then they calmed down and said they had escaped from the pen and that someone was following them and they couldn't let me out because I might be useful to them as a hostage."

The escapees followed 23rd Street to D Street and turned west, Godwin said. The car behind them apparently Newberry's turned east on D Street, she said. When Strickland and Fuston saw this they stopped near the Jason Lee Cemetery on D Street at Medical Center Drive, Godwin said. The man who was driving said, "We don't kill mothers," and the convicts released Godwin and continued west on D Street.

Salem police Lt. Charles Baker reported Godwin's car was found on Kenwood Street NE which runs north from State Street near 47th Avenue. An area resident called police after noticing the car parked on the street with its headlights on and the keys in the ignition since late afternoon. Baker said the car was apparently left there about 4:30 p.m. At least one of the men was seen walking west from that location. "We're not aware of any vehicles in the area that have been taken, so at this point we're assuming that they're on foot. Prison officials were certain that there was more than one inmate involved, penitentiary spokesman Al Chandler noted that several men would have been required to lift the couch concealing the escapees onto the flatbed truck in the prison upholstery shop. Strickland and Fuston were captured two days later, November 2, 1979 at the Calico Cat Motel in Tacoma Washington. Information on their whereabouts was furnished to police by a confidential informant. Both men surrendered and were returned to OSP

Before the escape Strickland was serving a life sentence on parole violation, burglary, robbery and kidnap charges from Harney and Douglas counties. He was described as an habitual criminal, with previous convictions on charges of kidnap, armed robbery, forgery, escape and assault, with intent to kill. The charges date back to 1956. Fuston was serving 20 years on 1978 Multnomah County convictions of parole violation, robbery and being an ex-convict in possession of a firearm He had served time previously for assault and robbery convictions.

Field Day Invitation Dated July 4th 1941 - Guests were invited to attend the events shown on page 84 of this book. Pass courtesy of Sergeant Tom Burke

Flax wagon with a false bottom, used in the escape of five inmates in April 1953
Five prisoners hid in the false bottom of a flax wagon, All five were recaptured, four at a roadblock near Newberg and a fifth in Vancouver, Washington,.

J.C. Verl Keeney
September 1, 1984 to August 1, 1986

J. C. Keeney was born July 16, 1934. He received a BA in 1957 from the College of Idaho and a MA in 1967 from OCE. He served two years in the U.S. Army, with an honorable discharge in 1959.

He went to work at OSCI in 1960 as recreation director. From 1963 to 1966 he served as a classroom teacher and from 1966 to 1968 as assistant principal. During that time he returned to college at OCE and obtained his masters degree. In 1968 he was appointed principal and served in that position one year. In 1969 he was appointed as director of rehabilitation programs at Oregon State Penitentiary. In 1972 J. C. Keeney was co-author of , "A Model for Adult Basic Education in Corrections." In 1974 he was co-author of, "A Model for Career Education in Corrections."

Photo OSP

In 1974 he was promoted to Assistant Superintendent.
In 1984 when Director of Corrections Bob Watson rotated the superintendents of all institutions he moved Hoyt Cupp to the central office in the position of inspector general. J. C. Keeney was promoted to the position of superintendent of OSP.

In 1986 he retired from OSP and moved to Arizona to work for the Arizona Department of Corrections. Keeney said it was Oregon's seemingly insoluble prison crowding problem that prompted him to look elsewhere. "We've been overcrowded for 10 years and nobody is doing anything about it," he said. He said, "the overwhelming defeat May 20 of a state prison bond issue was just the most recent in a series of such setbacks."

Number of employees November 27, 1984: 496

Number of inmates: OSP 1657

   Farm Annex   202

   Forest Camp   99

   Total: 1958

In 1984 the Death Penalty was restored in Oregon after seven years of litigation in the courts. Execution by lethal injection was adopted.

OSP Management Staff 1984-1986
Chaplain J. Jacobson, ?, D. Mills, M. Goraum, R. Hart, T. Crowley, C. Schnoor, C. Keaton, R. Martin, R. Helseth, S. Coleman, A. Kessiah, J. Seidler, , S. Gassner, J.C. Keeney, R. Chase, B. Chappelle, C. Reese, A. Santos, J. Muranaka, ?, C. Felker, S. Hill, ?, C. Stolpe, N. Armenakis, E. January, M. Collett; Front row: A. Chandler, K. Levitt, C. Beals, R. Inman.

New uniform patch designed
A uniform patch was adopted by the Department of Corrections with each institution having a rocker stripe above the patch with the name of the institution on it, circa 1991.

Rita Chase, a long time Executive Assistant to Superintendents from Hoyt Cupp to Brian Belleque

DOC Uniform Patch with OSP Rocker
Designed by C.O. Joe Pierre

Manfred (Fred) Maass
August 1, 1986 – June 30, 1994

Fred Maass was born in Berlin, Germany, June 2, 1939. He immigrated to the U.S. with his mother. He served in the U.S. Army and received an Honorable Discharge in 1962. He began his career in corrections as a correctional officer at Oregon State Penitentiary, November 9, 1964. He was working at the penitentiary during the riot of 1968. Maass served in a number of positions in the Department of Corrections: work release program representative, senior field representative, area supervisor, regional manager, deputy chief/parole and probation officer, parole and probation officer, social/support services manager — Oregon State Penitentiary, chief of release services — Department of Corrections Release Center, superintendent — Oregon State Penitentiary.

Photo courtesy OSP

During his management of OSP, eleven other prisons were constructed throughout the state of Oregon which doubled prison beds to 6,500. Many of the decisions regarding where an inmate would be assigned were up to the classification staff at OSP. Before the new institutions were ready for occupancy OSP was severely overcrowded, requiring daily review of case files to determine which inmates could be transferred or moved to minimum security facilities. A new intensive management unit was constructed on the grounds of OSP requiring oversight and added vigilance by OSP staff. A large portion of time was spent on legal issues involving petitions of review of disciplinary cases, federal civil rights and habeas corpus cases. Inmate health care issues included treatment for the aids virus and more inmates entering the prison with mental health problems.

During Maass's tenure at OSP the murder of Corrections Director Michael Francke occurred in the front driveway of the Dome Building, a few blocks from OSP, on the state hospital reservation. Frank Gable, a petty criminal from Salem, was convicted of aggravated murder in the Francke case, in what prosecutors said was a car theft gone bad. The ensuing investigations and subsequent appointment of a new Director of Corrections were stressful and time consuming. Staff morale issues were an ongoing challenge. Some institutions were represented by different bargaining units than OSP making inter institution transfers a bit more complex.

Maass retired in 1994 after a career in corrections serving in a variety of positions from corrections officer to superintendent. In retirement he has worked as a consultant on a variety of corrections issues. He is married to Helga Kasper and is the father of three children; Michael, Monica and Marcus Maass.. He received a BA degree from OCE in 1973 and an MS degree from WOSC in 1981

Number of inmates June 30, 1992: 1916
Number of employees: 442

"Inmates are in prison as punishment, not for punishment",
Fred Maass

OSP Management Staff 1986-1994
M.Hathaway, ?, ?H. Hammond, J. Forbes, C. Schnoor, T. Blaire, C. Keaton, D. Dawes, S. Coleman, R. Chase, F. Maass, ?, ?, Chaplain J. Jacobson, J. Muranaka, , A. Santos, D. Myers, R. Rice, ? , D. Mills, Row 3: R. Inman, R. Ross, T. Long, B. Stuhr, M. Goraum, Row 2; R. Martin, S. Gassner, N. Armenakis, R. Gorham, T. Crowley, Row 1; K. Levitt, L. Humbert, D. Andrews, M. Collett, C. Beals

DOC Cloth Patch
Photo: Jim Ramsey

DOC Badge
Photo: Jim Ramsey

Nick Armenakis
Acting Superintendent
July 1, 1994 through November 1994

For seven years Nick Armenakis was the assistant superintendent of Oregon State Penitentiary responsible for all of the security operations of the state's only maximum security prison. He routinely filled in as superintendent when necessary, including a 5-month stint as acting superintendent in 1994. He also played a key role in the design and operational start-up of the Intensive Management Unit, Oregon's super-max facility for maximum security inmates. Almost all of Mr. Armenakis's twenty two year professional career has been in corrections with the exception of a four-year tour of duty in the US Navy.

Nick Armenakis retired from DOC in December 2003.

Photo OSP

HONOR GUARD CO Mohler, CPL Hublitz, CO Peters, CPL Wallace, SGT Whitney, CO Pyle, CPL Cook, CO Bowser, CPL Hetlage, CO Weaver-Foster Photo OSP

S. Frank Thompson, Jr
December 1, 1994 to 1998

Frank Thompson received a BA degree in Social Welfare in 1969 from the University of Arkansas. He worked for the Arkansas Department of Corrections from August 1984 to November 1994 when he was appointed to the position at the Oregon State Penitentiary

The first execution in 34 years occurred September 6, 1996 at Oregon State Penitentiary. This process was presided over by Superintendent Thompson. The focus of public attention on this event was an additional challenge to Thompson.

Thompson is married to Deborah Hill Thompson and has a daughter.

Photo Sue Woodford

At the time of his appointment, overcrowding was the biggest problem facing the prison. Easing tensions caused by crowded conditions was a particular challenge. Relocating from Arkansas to Oregon becoming accustomed to a different state system, moving from a medium security institution with 800 inmates to a maximum security institution with over 2,000 inmates presented a formidable change for Thompson. Two pieces of legislation which became effective concurrent with his appointment were Measure 11 (Three Strikes and You are Out) requiring mandatory prison sentences for certain crimes and Measure 17 requiring prison inmates to participate 40 hours a week in work or training programs.

Number of Inmates: 2000 plus
Number of Employees:
Thompson left OSP in 1998 to serve as co-manager of the Central Institutions Operations Division with Nick Armenakis. Later Thompson was appointed Superintendent of Santiam Correctional Institution.

The Honor Guard was established under Fred Maass' tenure as Superintendant and continues to serve at ceremonial events

Mitch Morrow
Acting Superintendent
1998

Mitch Morrow joined the DOC in 1983 as a corrections officer at the penitentiary. Rising through the organization, he served as OSP's assistant superintendent of security and as acting superintendent of OSP in 1998 before becoming superintendent of OSCI later in 1998. Morrow was named administrator of Oregon Corrections Enterprises in 2001. He became DOC's Assistant Director for Institutions in 2002.

Morrow is a graduate of George Fox University and is pursuing a master's degree in business administration from George Fox University. He holds multiple certifications from the Department of Public Safety Standards and Training and the National Institute of Corrections.

Photo OSP

Sign describing the OSP emblem displayed at the front entrance to OSP
Photo: Sue Woodford

Joan Palmateer
April 1, 1998 – February 1, 2001

Joan Palmateer began her career in corrections at Oregon Women's Correctional Center as a correctional officer in 1980. She progressed there to corporal, sergeant, and security manager. She was also security manager and assistant superintendent at Oregon state correctional institution and Shutter Creek correctional institution. She is the first female superintendent of Oregon state penitentiary. She is a national authority on prison security and is a consultant with the National Institute of Corrections and the Federal Bureau of Prisons.

Palmateer has won numerous awards for her work in corrections including the Amos Reed Award for her leadership abilities. During her tenure at OSP the film "Bandits" was produced in the prison utilizing inmates and some staff members in the film.. The Oregon Film Commission awarded Palmateer

The 2000 Governor's Film Advocate Award, for her work on bringing the film to Oregon. One hundred and twenty five inmates appeared in the film as extras.

Photo OSP

Palmateer opened and staffed the newly constructed intensive management unit. This 196-bed, self-contained prison within a prison provides programs, housing and control for maximum-custody male inmates who are disruptive or who pose a substantial threat to staff and other inmates, as well as those inmates with a sentence of death

She is noted for her communication skills. While at OSP she paved the way for a more communicative and collaborative approach to doing business. She willingly spent time in the yard talking with inmates. She brought about changes in the operation of the yard by curtailing the practice of allowing all inmates in the yard at one time. The increase in incarceration of gang members and efforts on behalf of the administration to provide security for all those incarcerated and dispel nefarious activity by gangs led to regulated yard activity.

She spearheaded the drive to build a memorial to fallen officers. The memorial was completed and dedicated March 27, 2000.

Palmateer cited major challenges in supervising staff and inmates in a century old facility include safety, security, sanitation and solvency. She said the budget was never adequate enough to replace and repair the deteriorating physical plant and infrastructure. For years there has been a constant need for upgraded wiring, plumbing, emergency generators, modern cooking equipment, food service storage, and medical facilities. These problems with the physical plant never go away and the legislature is faced with making choices in how it divides up a finite pot of money between all state agencies. Spending money on prisons it not a popular choice. Palmateer made budget requests and lived with the funds appropriated.

The ongoing legal actions proliferated by inmates consumed staff time at all levels. Each level of staff is interviewed and reports written on every action taken resulting in a hearing or disciplinary action involving an inmate. Appeals and grievances and the resulting investigations required in each step of this process further consumed the time of the superintendent.

In April 1999, OSP became one of the few prisons in the U.S. to initiate a hospice program for terminally ill patients. The much-acclaimed program won the National Commission on Correctional Health Care's 2001 Program of the Year Award in recognition of its "proactive role" in preparing individuals and the system to deal with dying inmates, and in helping those inmates to experience humane, comfortable and dignified deaths." OSP Health Services Manager, William Cahal, RN, BS, CCHP, spearheaded the program whereby inmates were trained as hospice volunteers to assist terminally ill inmate patients. The Hospice at OSP became a national model when it was selected as a demonstration site for the GRACE Project. (A Volunteers of America initiative promoting high quality end of life care for terminally ill inmates.) *NCCHC Newsletter*

Number of inmates; 2200
Number of employees: 560

Joan Palmateer has served as superintendent of Coffee Creek Correctional Facility and Department of Corrections population management administrator. In 2008 she was appointed assistant director of facility operations, Oregon Youth Authority

Memorial to fallen officers dedicated March 27, 2000.
Photo Sue Woodford

Stan Czerniak
February 2001 – September 30, 2002

Stan W. Czerniak was born in Brainerd, Minnesota. He later lived in Texas and Illinois. After high school he served in Vietnam achieving the rank of Sergeant E 5. He was awarded the Bronze Star Medal, Cross of Gallantry, Ranger Badge and other citations.

Czerniak holds a master's degree in administration from George Williams College and a bachelor's degree in sociology/psychology from Aurora University, both in Illinois. After graduation from college he began a twenty plus year career in corrections. His career began with work in juvenile corrections and in recent years has focused on adult corrections primarily in administration.

He was appointed superintendent of the Oregon Sate Penitentiary February 1, 2001 and served in that capacity until September 30, 2002 when he accepted a position as Assistant Director of Corrections for Operations.

Photo OSP

After the September 11, 2001 attack on the twin towers in New York City, the OSP veterans association asked Czerniak for permission to purchase and install a flag pole in the prison yard. He granted their request and this plaque was presented to him. He says it is one of the most memorable events at OSP.

VETERANS ASSOCIATION
Oregon State Penitentiary

SQUADRON APPRECIATION AWARD

PRESENTED TO:

STAN W. CZERNIAK
Superintendent
Oregon State Penitentiary

In Recognition Of Your Continuing Support And Assistance To The Veterans Association.
It Is With Heartfelt Appreciation That We Thank You For Supporting Our Request To Raise The American Flag Inside Of This Facility.

January 18, 2002

Brian Belleque
May 16, 2003- present

Brian Belleque, a corrections veteran who began his career as a correctional officer June 6, 1983 at OSP. He, worked both at the penitentiary and Oregon state correctional institution in Salem. His background in prison security and correctional programs, and service as acting superintendent of the penitentiary since August 2002 prepared him for the position. He succeeded Stan Czerniak who was promoted to administrator of the department's Institutions Division. Belleque graduated from Southern Oregon University, holds several certifications from the Oregon Department of Public Safety Standards and Training, and has served as a consultant for the National Institute of Corrections.

Significant events that had an impact on Belleque's management of OSP include the passage of ballot measure 11 also known as "three strikes and you are out." This measure for the majority of inmates eliminated the ability to earn good time credits. The passage of ballot measure 17 had another negative impact on prison management in that it requires inmates to work forty hours per week. Finding jobs for two thousand three hundred and six inmates and a place to perform them in a one hundred fifty year old maximum security prison with a deteriorating infrastructure and a finite amount of space is a questionable mandate.

Photo: OSP

Budget reductions in programs in 2002 and 2003 resulted in the elimination of the GED (General Equivalency Diploma) and ABE (Adult Basic Education) programs. These programs slowly came back in 2006. Another major management issue of this period was the severe increase in security threat inmates (gangs). The gangs are characterized with aggressive self centered behavior with lack of consideration of other inmates. They are a danger to themselves and staff and require skilled extraction techniques in moving them from one area to another. Lacking the ability to receive "good time" credits , these inmates have little to lose in assaulting other, weaker inmates

Belleque has sought to recognize and respect the history and success of OSP and to move it progressively forward in order to assist the Department of Corrections in meeting it's mission.

In 2009 many areas of the institution have critical needs, i.e., newer technology, a more sophisticated locking system, as well as electrical and computer system upgrades. More appropriately designed cell houses are needed to accommodate the growing gang populations. The legislature has provided funding to the Mental Health Division for the construction of new hospital facilities for the criminally insane. The Oregon State Prison has many mentally ill inmates committed to their custody. A modern facility is needed to house these individuals apart from the general prison population.

The knowledge, skills and abilities of the position of superintendent has changed dramatically since 1866 when the first prison was opened in Oregon.

Number of employees: 450
Number of inmates: 2,306

Home of superintendents through the administration of Hoyt Cupp is located on the OSP grounds.
Photo: Sue Woodford

OSP Uniform patch in use in 1970, 1980, 1990

"On your next trip to Salem, visit the Penitentiary Curio Store"
Advertisement in the 1964 Shadows publication

In 1906 the inmates produced button hooks, hair bridal whips and books of poetry for sale to visitors as described in the book "Prison Tours and Poems" by inmate Van Tiffin #4382

Landmark Closed
The prison curio shop was closed when State Street was widened.
"Because of the flood in 1996, the city had to install a four foot tall levy across the area and in order to put the curio shop back in, they would have had to elevate it 74 inches and have all the utilities re-constructed." *Minutes Capitol Projects Advisory Board –– July 16, 2004. Photo: Ed Ben*

Carl Beals and Sue Woodford-Beals at OSP February 22, 2007. Photo: Mike Yoder

Authors

Carl Beals worked for Oregon State Penitentiary for 30 years. He began his career as a correctional officer and after graduation from Western Oregon State University advanced to counseling and retired as Manager of Social and Psychological Services. He is a native Oregonian. He and Woodford were married in the OSP Chapel by Reverend Jim Jacobson.

Sue Woodford-Beals graduated from Marylhurst University. She has worked for federal, regional, county and state government. Her corrections career includes work for the State Board of Parole, Oregon State Penitentiary and she retired as Manager of Support Services for Santiam Correctional Institution.

Genealogy research is a hobby for the couple. Woodford-Beals is a member of the Daughters of the American Revolution, and Daughters of the Confederacy. Both are members of the Willamette Valley Genealogy Society. In 1981 they assisted in founding the Oregon State Association of Corrections Retirees.

Thanks to the Department of Corrections and Oregon State Penitentiary Superintendents for their cooperation on this project.

End Notes

1. Hubert Howe Bancroft, *History of Oregon Vol II, 1848-1888 p. 645*
2. *Report of Penitentiary Commissioners, May 31, 1865*
3. *"The Oregon Penitentiary"* Oregon Statesman Newspaper August 20, 1866
4. *Superintendent Shaw Report to Governor George L. Woods, September 1866*
5. *First Biennial Report of the State Board of Charities and Corrections, December 31, 1892 p. 263*
6. *"Operations and Conditions of the State Penitentiary"* American Unionist Newspaper Salem, Oregon, Monday, Dec. 9, 1867
7. *Report of the Superintendent of the State Penitentiary to the Fifth Regular Session, September 1868*
8. *Superintendent Berry's Report to Governor George L. Woods, September 1, 1868 p. 849*
9. *Ibid p. 36*
10. *"Bits for Breakfast"*, Salem Statesman. January 21, 1933, p. 94
11. *The State of Oregon Illustrated History 1873 edition p. 994*
12. *Ibid p. 994*
13. *Biennial Report of Superintendent Burch to Governor S.F. Chadwick, September 1, 1878*
14. *"Minister Braved Racist Back Lash"*, Capi Lynn, Statesman Journal, February 26, 2007
15. *"The Bush Family, Asahel Bush II"*, Anne M. Powell
16. *Biennial Report of Superintendent Bush to Governor W.W. Thayer, November 1, 1878 to August 31, 1880*
17. *Biennial Report of Superintendent Stratton to Governor Z. F. Moody September 1, 1882 to Sept. 7, 1884*
18. *Biennial Report of Superintendent Collins to Governor Z. F. Moody, January 1, 1885 to Dec. 31, 1886*
19. *Ibid*
20. *Biennial Report of Superintendent Downing to Governor Sylvester Pennoyer, Jan. 1887 to Dec. 31, 1888*
21. *Report of Superintendent Downing to Governor Sylvester Pennoyer, March 9, 1895*
22. *Report of Prison Physician E.B. Philbrook, M.D., to Superintendent A. N. Gilbert, January 31, 1897*
23. *Biennial Report of Superintendent Gilbert to Governor William P. Lord March 11, 1895 to April 1, 1899*
24. *Escapes and Captures Report of Superintendent Lee to Governor T. T. Geer, October 1, 1902*
25. *Biennial Report of Superintendent Lee to Governor T.T. Geer, October 1, 1902*
26. *Ibid, p.11*
27. *Biennial message of T.T. Geer to the Twenty Second Legislative Assembly 1903*
28. *Penitentiary Staff of Superintendent C. W. James*
29. *"Governor takes bit in his teeth, takes charge of the Penitentiary"* Daily Statesman, May 6, 1912
30. *"Governor Oswald West's report to the Legislature"* Daily Statesman, January 11, 1911
31. *"Bogus Coin Made in Prison"* Daily Capitol Journal, August 8, 1912
32. *Biennial Report of Superintendent Curtis to Governor Oswald West, October 1, 1912*
33. *Biennial Report of Superintendent Lawson to the Oregon Board of Parole October 4, 1914, p.105*
34. *Ibid p. 105*
35. *"Hundreds Honor Slain Official"* The Daily Oregon Statesman Newspaper, September 30, 1915 p.4
36. *"Oregon State Penitentiary"* Harry P. Minto, Superintendent, The Oregon Bluebook 1913-1914 p. 93
37. *Twenty Fifth Biennial Report of the Oregon State Penitentiary from Superintendent John W. Minto to the Board of Control*
38. *Twenty Sixth Biennial Report of the Oregon State Penitentiary for the period ending Sept.30, 1918 by Charles A. Murphy Superintendent to Governor James Withycombe*
39. *Ibid*
40. *"The Oregon State Penitentiary"* Robert L. Stevens, Superintendent, The Oregon Bluebook 1917-1918
41. *The Oregon State Penitentiary*, R E L Steiner, Superintendent, The Oregon Bluebook 1919-1920

Acknowledgments

For many years our friends and colleagues in corrections have lamented the lack of a formal history of the Oregon State Penitentiary and the dedicated people who managed its operation. We wish to acknowledge all the many people who assisted us in compiling this history of the prison.

OSP staff and families: John and Marge Akin, Shirley and B.J. Adams, Wayne & Diana Baker, Edmund and Delores Ben, Brian Belleque, Jerry Bryans, Kris and Tom Burke, Chuck and Sue Choat, David M. Dowell, Vance and Shirley Gwynn, Keith and LaVelle Gwynn, Lloyd and Evelyn Hamby, Ron and Lois Haskins, Don and Maxine Johnson, Dave and Edna Karn, Charlie Keaton, Hal and Lily Lindstrom, Ted Long, Fred and Helga Maass, David Meyerhofer, John Nolan, Nina Novak, Stan and Gail Perry, Jim Ramsey, Marvin and Caroline Reece, Carl and Lou Reinwald, Rollin Smedstad, Vern and Peggy Spitz, Gary and Kay Stark, Lyle and Virginia Suiter, L. L. Sullivan, Virgil Taylor, David Trent, Don Versteeg, Harol and Wanda Whitley, Dick Wenger, Pete Weigel,

Others who have helped in this project: Leroy Barker, Attorney, Historian Alaska State Bar, Carole Healey, Angie Delmoral; Sitka, Alaska, Merrialyce Blanchard, Reference Librarian, Oregon State Library, David Wendell, Oregon State Archives, Liza Dormady Manager/Curator, Portland Police Historical Society, Kathy Milner, Portland Oregon

Gas Chamber building 1952 After the execution of Wayne Long in August 1952 the gas chamber was moved to this new location inside the walls adjacent to the Isolation and Segregation building. The first executions in this building were; Frank Payne, Morris Leland and Albert Karnes in January 1953. The structure on the roof is not an antennae, but support for the vertical pipe that exhausts the gas from the chamber. Photo: Grant Yoder

Index

Acme Thunderer Whistle 27
Adams, Laura M. 23
Adams, Shirley & B.J. 123
Akin, Marge & John 123
Alaska 12
Alaskan Newspaper 13
Alexander, George Cassie 3 6 83–84
Allard, Seth 7
Amstutz, Roy 99
Andrews, D 111
Armenakis, N. 105 109 111
Armenakis, Nick 112
Assistant Warden 27
Asylum, Oregon Insane 45
Atkinson, George 7
Authors 121
Badge, Assistant Yard Captain 96
Badge, OSP hat 97
Badge: Assistant Captain of Yard Badge 96
Badge: Chapel Guard Badge of Don Johnson 96
Badge: OSP Oldest Hat Badge 96
Baker, Diana & Wayne 123
Baker, Lt. Charles 107
Ball, Colonel 13
Baxter, Bruce 78
Beals, C. E. 105 109 111 121
Belcrest Cemetery 70
Belknap, D.H. 1
Belleque, Brian 3 6 109 118–120 123
Ben, Ed 91 98 120
Ben, Edmund & Delores 123
Benson, J J. 49
Bernt, F. 105
Berry, James 45
Berry, Major Montgomery P. 6 11–13
Berry, Sarah Isabella 11
Berry, Winnie Silvers 12
Bertillion System 34
Blaire, T. 111
Bligh, Frank 62
Bligh, T.G. 62
Board of Control 5 87
Bonny Watson Memorial Park Mausoleum 24
Bowles, W. 105
Bowser, CO 112
Boy's Training School Cemetery 104
Boyd, Rosalie 43
Brodie, E.E. 51
Brown, Emma Murphy 55
Brown, Martin V. 17
Brudos, J. 149
Brunk House. 8
Bryans, Jerry 123
Burch, Benjamin F. 3 6 19–20
Burch, Samuel 20
Bureau of Criminal Identification 38

Burke, Kris & Tom 123
Burke, Sergeant Tom 81 96 97 137 138
Burkett, Mrs 89
Burkhart, Sam 49
Burns., Elizabeth 28
Bush, Asahel 3 6
Bush House 22
Bush Pasture Park 22
Butler, Lawson David Shirk 85
Cahal, William 116
Calico Cat Motel 107
Canemah 22
Capitan, Vincent 148
Caponette, Mary 104
Carson, Joseph K. 48
Cemetery, State Boys Training School 145
Cemetery inside OSP 146
Chandler 109
Chapman, Rhoda 74
Chappelle, B. 105 109
Chase, Amanda Blanche 103
Chase, R. 109 111
Chatten, Esther Collins 26
Choat, Sue & Chuck 123
City View Cemetery 65 78
Clarke, Samuel Asahel 15
Clatawed., Charley 8
Cleveland, Grover 20
Clow, George 26
Coffee Creek Correctional Facility 5
Coleman, S. 105 109 111
Collett, M. 109 111
Collins, George 3 6 25–27 26
Columbia River Correctional Institution 5
Compton, David R. 62
Compton, Gresham M. 62
Compton, Louis H. 6
Compton, Louis Hartt 62–64
Cook, CPL 112
Correctional Classification Board 99
Corwin, Faye 83
Creffield, Franz E. 45
Crites, Mary J. 62
Crowley, . 111
Crowley, T. 105 109
Cupp, Benjamin 104
Cupp, Clara 104
Cupp, Cynthia 104
Cupp, Hoyt Carl 3 6 87 101 103–105
Cupp, Theodore Judd 103
Cupp, Thomas 104
Curry, George L. 1
Curtis, Charles 46
Curtis, Frank Hamilton 6 46 47
Curtis, Hamilton 42
Curtis, Lillian 41

Curtis, Thomas 46
Czerniak, Stan 3·6·117
Dallas City Cemetery 69
Dalrymple, Amos 3·71
Dalrymple, Amos M. 6·68–70
Dalrymple, Denton F. 68
Dalrymple, Hamilton Sherman 68
Dalrymple, Jim 15
Dalton,B.H. 34
Davidson, Eliza Ann 19
Dawes, D. 111
Dawes, Debra Martin 104
Dayton, Winifred 65·78
DeAutremont brothers 70
Deer Ridge Correctional Facility 5
Dilley, Frank 146
Doland, W.P. 1
Dome Building 27
Dowell,David M. 123
Downing, Alexander 28
Downing, George 3
Downing, George S. 6·28–30
Eades, Ellen 74
Eades, George A. Eades. George 74
Eastern Oregon Correction Institution 5
Eastern Star Home 55
Eckrode, B. 105
Eddon, Jane 12
End Notes 122–125
English, Levi 1
Epeneter, Dr. 99
Escaped Prisoners Booklet 1916 53
Escaped Prisoners Booklet 1924 70
Escape From Inside OSP 106
Evans, Missouri 29
Everetts, W. 105
Executions 129
Executions, 1851-2009 131
Farm Annex 5
Felker, C 105 109
Ferrell, Frank 34
Film Projection Room 64
Fiskum, Dave 107
Fitch, A.D. 1
Flax Operation 74
Flege, Earl C. 60
Folger Adams Key 97
Folquet, Maurice 85
Forbes, J. 111
Foundry buildings 64
Francke, Michael 110
Fritte, Raymond 94
Fry, D.J. 59
Fry, Dan 60
Fuston, Delbert 106
Gable, Frank 110
Gaddis, Thomas 87
Gale, J. M. 11

Gallows, Oregon State Penitentiary 39
Gas Chamber 86
Gas Chamber building 123
Gas chamber photo 130
Gassner, S. 105·109·111
Geer, T.T. 34
Gilbert, Andrew 3
Gilbert, Andrew Nathan 6
Gilbert, James 31
Gilliam, Colonel 19
Gladden, C.T. 3
Gladden, Clarence T. 6
Gladden, Clarence Theron 87–98
Gladden, Emma T. 87
Gladden, George 87
Gladden, Isaac 87
Gladden, Margaret 88
Godwin, Debra 106
Goff, Ethel 71
Golden, Belle 59
Goraum, M. 105·109·111
Gorham, R. 111
Governor George Curry Letter 139
Grant, U.S. 12
Grant County Historical Society 14
Grover, LaFayette 17
Guards Quarters 92
Guards Quarters Diningroom 93
Gwynn, Keith & Lavelle 123
Gwynn, Vance & Shirley 123
Haag, Doris M. 104
Hamby, Lloyd & Evelyn 123
Hamilton, Jennie 25
Hamilton, Lucinda M. 46
Hammond, H 111
Handcuffs 91
Hart, R. 105·109
Harvey, Ellen 73
Haskins, Ron & Lois 123
Hass, Elizabeth 59
Hastings, Lucius 1·5
Hathaway, M 111
Hayes, Ace 87
Heartbreak Hotel 92
Helseth, R. 109
Hempy, Nancy E. 85
Henry, M. 105
Herren family 104
Hetlage, CPL 112
Hill, Deborah 113
Hill, S. 105·109
Hill Top Cemetery 20
Hixon, Mary Emily 15
Hobbs, Fern 47
Hobson Whitney Cemetery 12
Holman, Adelaide 68
Holman, Hardy 68
Holman, J.M. 68

Holman, Margaret 68
HONOR GUARD 112
Hooker, Otto 49
Hopper, Sarah 34
Hospital, Oregon State 32
Hoss, Hal E. 73
Hot Lake Sanatorium 71
Hublitz, CPL 112
Humbert, L. 111
Hurst, Margaret 31
Hurt, Maud 45
Hurt, Molly 45
Inman, R. 105·109·111
Inmate art program 148
Inmate Baseball Team 48
Isolation and Segregation building 144
Jackson, Bennie 146
Jacobson, J. 105·109·111
James, Charles W. 3·6·41–44
James, Myrta 43
James, Rosalia 41
James, Roscoe 43
James, Winfrey 41
January, E. 109
Johns, Sylvia 68
Johnson, Don & Maxine 123
Johnson, Joe Sergeant 143
Johnson, Walt 49
Johnston, Emma 47
Jones, Bert "Oregon" 68
Jones, Thurston 34
Kahle, L. 105
Kane, William 14
Karn, Dave 105 136
Karn, Dave & Edna 123
Kay, Thomas B. 73
Keaton, C. 105·109·111
Keaton, Charlie 123
Keeney, J. C. 3·6·105·109
Keeney, J.C.Verl 108–109
Kessiah, A. 109
King, William 1
Kitchen OSP 63
Ladd & Tilton Bank 57
Ladd, W.S. 1·21
Ladd, William 57
Lamb, Charity 8·10
Lamb, William E. 40
Lamourex, H. L. 55
Lawson, Berton K. 3·6·46·47
Lawson, Foster 47
Lee, Joseph Daniel 3 6 34–39
Lee, Nicholas 34
Lee Mission Cemetery 26
Lethal Injection table photo 135
Levitt, K. 109·111
Lewis, James W 6 65 77–82
Lewis, John Harrison 65

Lillie, Charles 71
Lillie, John William "Will" 3·6·71–72
Lilly, Jordan Belle 48
Lincoln Cemetery 35
Lincoln Memorial Park 72
Lindstrom, Hal & Lily 123
Little, D. 149
Lobby, OSP i
Long, J. L. 49
Long, Ted 111 123
Lonsdale, D.H. 1·5
Los Angeles Veterans National Cemetery 62
Maass, Fred & Helga 123
Maass, Manfred (Fred) 3 6 110–111
Maass, Marcus 110
Maass, Michael 110
Maass, Monica 110
MacLaren School for Boys 99
Martin, Charles H. 77
Martin, R. 105·109·111
Marwood, William 14
McCall, Tom Lawson
McConnell, Francis L. 85
McCormick, S.J. 1
McCully, David 31
McCully, Estelle 32
McKay, Douglas
McNary, Dr. 26
McNary, Sarah 8
McNary, Sarah Eleanor 7
McRae, Hiram 146
Means, Martha Ann 65
Memorial to fallen officers 116
Merrill, David 34
Meyerhofer, David 123
Meyers, Henry W. 6·73–76
Meyers, Joseph 73
Meyers, M. L. 73
Miles Linen Mill 73
Miller Mercantile Co 73
Mills, D. 109·111
Milne, Kathy 11·123
Minto, Doug 50
Minto, Harry Percy 3 6 49–50
Minto, Jasper (Jap) 26
Minto, John W. 3·6·51–53
Minto, Laura 51
Mitchell, Donna 45
Mitchell, Esther 45
Mitchell, George 45
Mohler, CO 112
Moore, Sandra 104
Moores, J. H. 7
Morrison, Martha Ann 49
Morrow, Mitch 114
Morse, W. B. 11
Morton, G. 105
Mt. Crest Abbey Mausoleum 29·33·61

Index

Mulke, F.W. 51
Muranaka 111
Muranaka, J. 109
Murphy, Charles A. 6, 54–55
Murphy, Sarah E. 54
Murphy, William P. 54
Murray, Joe 38, 39, 53, 70
Murray, Joe S. 81
Myers, D 111
Myers, H.C. 25
Nagel, S. 148
Newall, Robert 1
New Tacoma Cemetery 88
Nolan, John 123
Norris, Shubrick 1
Novak, Nina 123
O'Brien, James 146
O'Bryant, Hugh 1, 5
O'Malley, Patricia 85
O'Malley, Peter J. 85
O'Malley, Terrance 85
O'Malley, Virgil J. 6, 85
Odell Lake 12
Old wall 95
Oliver, Jerry 148
Oregon's Forgotten Children 146
Oregon Insane Asylum 25, 27
Oregon Memorabilia 81
Oregon Mounted Riflemen. 19
Oregon Prison Association
Oregon Prison Map 147
Oregon Reform School 43
Oregon State Hospital 59
Oregon State Penitentiary 5
Oregon Women's Correctional Center 10
Oregon Womens Correctional Center 5
Oregon Womens Corrections Center 87
OSP Emblem Credit 114
OSP Postcard 1910 56
Palmateer, Joan 3, 6, 115–116
Parker, S. 1
Parker, Theodore C. 12
Parrish, J. L. 22
Partridge, W. M. 13
Patton, Hal D. 41, 43
Perry, Stan & Gail 123
Peters, CO 112
Peyton, Anna 62
Pierre, J 109
Pinson, John 85
Pioneer Cemetery 22, 55, 74, 104
Pioneer Cemetery Hillsboro 84
Poe, "Buck" Dupree 85
Portland Evening Telegram Newspaper 36
Portland Memorial 51, 57
Powder River Correctional Facility 5
Powell, Martha L. 23
Power Generation Plant 69
Pray, Charles 78
Prigg Cottage 5
Prison Farm Annex 43
Prison Officers Baseball team 92
Prison Tours and Poems 18
Pyle, CO 112
Ramsey, Jim 123
Randall, George W. 89
Randall, George Washington 87, 89
Records Office 89
Recreation Yard Gate 61
Recreation Yard OSP photo 142
Reece, Marvin & Caroline 123
Reese, C. 109
Reinwald, Carl & Lou 123
Rice, R. 111
Riot damage 90
Riverview Cemetery 48
Roach, L. 105
Robnett, J. H. 55
Rose City Cemetery 46
Ross, R 111
Ross, R. 111
Rossiter, Elizabeth A. 29
Russell, Josephine Llewellyn 71
Sacred Heart Academy 11
Salem American Unionist 11
Salem Pioneer Cemetery 50
Santos, A. 109, 111
Savage, George 65
Savage, Morgan L. 7
Schnoor, C. 109, 111
Schuck, B. 105
Schucking, Agnes Gilbert 32
Schumacher, D. 105
Scroggins, Loma 8
Seed, R. 105
Seidle, J. 105
Seidler, J. 109
Sharpe, Bertha V. 62
Shaw, Alva Compton Riggs 6, 7–10
Shaw, Joshua 7
Shiel, Colonel 21
Shoe Shop, OSP 58
Shutter Creek Correctional Facility 5
Simmons, Flora M. 55
Sitka 12
Sitka National Cemetery. 12
Sloane, Joseph 1
Smedstad, Roland 123
Smetana, G. 105
Smith, Asa C. 67
Smith, C. Kate 31
Smith, Johnson 3
Smith, Johnson S. 6
Smith, Mary Evans 29
Smith, Richard 89
Smith, Robert W. 67

Snake River Correctional Institution 5
Southern Steel Key 97
Spangrud, D. 105
Spitz, Vern & Peggy 123
Stadter, Dorothy 84
Stadter, Edward O. 84
Stark, Gary & Kay 123
State Board of Parole and Probation 99
State Police Badge 81
State Reform School 12
State Training School for Boys 5·43·76
Steiner, Gideon 59
Steiner, Milton B. 60
Steiner, Robert E. Lee 3·6·59–60
Steiners Drug Store 59
Stevens, Robert L. 3·6·57–58
Stolpe, C 109
Stone, Stephen A. 40·81
Stratton, Curtis P. 23
Stratton, Julius 3·28
Stratton, Julius A. 6
Stratton, Julius Adams 24
Stratton, Lavinia Fitch 23
Stratton, Riley 24
Street Car to Prison vi
Strickland, Wayne 106
Stuhr, B. 111
Suiter, Lyle & Virginia 123
Sullivan, Kate 51
Sullivan, L.L. 123
Superintendents office 72
Sweeney, John 68
Taylor, Virgil 123
Theater in the OSP dining room
Thompson, S. Frank 3 6 113
Tiffany, Baily T. 34
Tour donation box ii
Tracy, Harry 34
Trent, David 123
Tuberculosis Sanitarian 92
Two Rivers Correctional Institution 5
Umscheid, Michael 148
Uniform buttons 82
Uniforms 97
Uniforms 1850-1980 137
Uniforms 1980-2008 138
Uniform single breasted brass buttons 88
VanDeusen, Edwin R. 57
Van Tiffen 18
Van Tiffin 120
Versteeg, Don 123
Wade, John 34
Wallace, CPL 112
Warner Creek Correctional Facility 5
Watkinds, William H. 3·6·15–16·19·25
Watson, Bob 108
Way, Barry 14
Weaver-Foster, CO 112

Weber, M. 105
Weigel, Merle "Pete" 123·138
Wendel, Charlotte 84
Wenger, Dick 123
Wentworth, L.T. 51
West, Oswald 41·43
Whistle, Acme Thunderer 27
Whitaker, John 1
White, W. J. 41
White Corner General Store 73
Whitley, H. 105
Whitley, Harol 101
Whitley, Harol & Wanda 123
Whitney, SGT 112
Wilcox, Theodore Burney 57
Williams, C. 105
Wilson, Tom 41
Witten, Eliza Alice 34
Womens Release Unit 5
Womens Ward inmates 76
Woodford-Beals, Sue 121
Woods, George L. 11
Woods, Louisa 11
Worrell, Samuel 56
Yocum, Rebecca H. 51
Young Men's Christian Association 62
Zieber, Eugenia 22

Executions in Oregon

Historically the ultimate disapproval of behavior unacceptable by the majority has been banishment, incarceration and/or execution.

There has always been a need to have a process that is equitable to all who are accused of deviation from the norm or violation of the laws of the land.

Execution in Oregon has been voted in and out then back in over the last one hundred fifty years of Oregon's history.

The methods of execution in Oregon has included the following:

1. Shooting (Before 1850)

2. Hanging

3. Asphyxiation (Gas Chamber)

4. Lethal Injection

These four methods are shown in the following chart of legal executions in Oregon from 1850 through 1996.

The first executions listed occurred as a result of the Whitman Massacre. Natives listed were indicted and a true bill issued by jurors signed by F. W. Pettygrove, Forman of the jury November 29, 1847.

These early executions in the county's of conviction have carried with them a bizarre circus like atmosphere. It was for this reason in 1903 the law was amended by the Oregon Legislature mandating all executions to occur within the walls of the Oregon State Penitentiary in Salem.

The first such execution was not without problems and notoriety. Initially the execution went according to the rules and guidelines set down by the governing body. The problem occurred when the remains of the decedent Harry Egbert aka Jack Frost, were sent to an Oregon Medical School. "An enterprising but conscienceless student removed the skin from the lifeless body and tanned it into pliable and velvety leather." "He passed the word down the line that strips of it would be for sale in a few days and the demand exceeded the supply." "A great many of the uncanny bits of hide are in the possession of prominent people, who seem to highly prize their ghastly mementos." Both men and women in Salem are reported to have obtained the items which were described in the April 9, 1904 issue of the Daily Capitol Journal newspaper in Salem titled, "Grasping Grim Curios."

In 1951 when Virgil O'Malley was appointed superintendent of OSP he arranged for the construction of a concrete block building to be built outside the OSP walls on the back side of the reservation. The purpose of this building was to house the gas chamber which previously had been located on the second floor of the prison. The inmate executed August 12, 1952 in this new building was Wayne Long. Those present at the execution report that shortly thereafter the superintendent learned that it was not legal for an execution to occur outside the prison walls. The chamber was then moved back inside the walls and housed in a building on the ground floor of the then segregation and isolation building outside of the building but within the walls.

The previously constructed concrete building known as "O'Malley's Folly" was turned into a paint storage building. Records show that prior to his execution Wayne Long had dinner in the superintendent's office and played cards with the guards. His only visit outside the walls during his incarceration was the ride from the prison to the chamber.

The lethal injection method of execution was used in the execution of Douglas Wright and Harry Moore in 1996 and 1997 both men refused to appeal their convictions. According to the Oregon Department of Corrections, "Douglas Wright's execution cost the taxpayers of Oregon nearly $200,000.00. Although Wright chose not to pursue any of the legal appeals available to him, approximately $90,000 was expended on legal fees to fend off third-party law suits, and $85,000 for staff overtime for training and security duties." These two executions were the last ones to occur in Oregon, however, many inmates are currently housed on death row awaiting execution.

"The only woman ever to be sentenced to death in Oregon, had her sentence commuted in 1964 when Oregon voters repealed the death penalty. Jeannace Freeman, a 20 year old white waitress was convicted of murdering her female lover's (Gertrude Nunez) young son by throwing him off the bridge in Jefferson County into the Crooked River Gorge."

The Gas chamber was used in Oregon from 1938 until August 20, 1962. Photo: OSP

Executions in Oregon 1851 to 2009

NAME	AGE	RACE	SEX	OCCUPATION	CRIME	METHOD	DATE
TILAUKAIT		NAT. AMER.	MALE		MURDER	HANGING	JUN 2 1850
THOMAHAS		NAT AMER	MALE		MURDER	HANGING	JUN 2 1850
KIASUMPKIN		NAT AMER	MALE		MURDER	HANGING	JUN 2 1850
KLOKOMOS		NAT. AMER.	MALE		MURDER	HANGING	JUN 2 1850
ISAIACHALAKIS		NAT. AMER.	MALE		MURDER	HANGING	JUN 2 1850
KENDALL, WILLIAM		WHITE	MALE	FARMER	MURDER	HANGING	APR 18 1851
TURNER, CREED		WHITE	MALE	CATTLEMAN	MURDER	HANGING	DEC 4 1851
EVERMAN, RETURN	22	WHITE	MALE	CARPENTER	MURDER	HANGING	MAY 11 1852
WIMPLE, ADAM	37	WHITE	MALE	FARMER	MURDER	HANGING	JAN 8 1852
ROE, CHARLES		WHITE	MALE	TRAPPER	MURDER	HANGING	1859
BALCH, DANFORD	47	WHITE	MALE	FARMER	MURDER	HANGING	JAN 17 1859
MOSS, MATTHEW		WHITE	MALE		MURDER	HANGING	MAR 20 1860
GEORGE, PHILIP		WHITE	MALE	BOARDING HSE OWN	MURDER	HANGING	JUN 22 1860
PATE, ANDREW		WHITE	MALE		MURDER	HANGING	MAY 27 1862
GRIFFITH, ZEBULON		WHITE	MALE	BLACKSMITH	MURDER	HANGING	JUN 9 1863
BEALE, GEORGE		WHITE	MALE	SALOON KEEPER	MURDER-ROBBERY	HANGING	MAY 17 1865
BAKER, GEORGE		WHITE	MALE	BUTCHER	MURDER-ROBBERY	HANGING	MAY 17 1865
CAIN, WILLIAM		WHITE	MALE	MINER	MURDER	HANGING	AUG 3 1865
SMITH, THOMAS		WHITE	MALE		MURDER	HANGING	MAY 10 1866
BLACK, JIM		NAT. AMER	MALE		MURDER	HANGING	JAN 3 1873
SCHONCHIN, JOHN		NAT. AMER.	MALE		MURDER	HANGING	JAN 3 1873
KINTPUASH		NAT. AMER.	MALE	CHIEF	MURDER	HANGING	JAN 3 1873
BOSTON, CHARLEY		NAT. AMER.	MALE		MURDER	HANGING	JAN 3 1873
LEWIS, SEVIER	52	WHITE	MALE	FARMER	MURDER	HANGING	AUG 30 1878
OWL, WHITE	35	NAT. AMER.	MALE		MURDER	HANGING	JAN 10 1879
QUIT-A-TUMPS		NAT. AMER.	MALE		MURDER	HANGING	JAN 10 1879

APS	30	NAT. AMER.	MALE		MURDER	HANGING	JAN 18 1879
COOK, JAMES		WHITE	MALE	CONVICT	MURDER	HANGING	FEB 7 1879
AVERY, EUGENE	25	WHITE	MALE	EX CONVICT	MURDER	HANGING	MAR 14 1879
JOHNSON, JAMES	25	WHITE	MALE	EX CONVICT	MURDER	HANGING	MAR 14 1879
KAT, KOO		NAT. AMER.	MALE		MURDER	HANGING	MAY 5 1879
AH, LEE		ASIAN	MALE	LABORER	MURDER	HANGING	APR 20 1880
MURPHY, ARTHUR	31	WHITE	MALE	SHEPHERD	MURDER	HANGING	JAN 5 1881
KAT-AT-CHA		NAT. AMER.	MALE		MURDER	HANGING	MAR 28 1882
ROGERS, CHARLES		WHITE	MALE	PRISON GUARD	MURDER	HANGING	JAN 28 1885
MURRAY, J., W.		WHITE	MALE		MURDER	HANGING	FEB 13 1885
DRAKE, JOSEPH		BLACK	MALE	FARM LABORER	MURDER	HANGING	MAR 20 1885
ONEIL, LOUIS		WHITE	MALE		MURDER	HANGING	MAR 12 1886
MARPLE, RICHARD	27	WHITE	MALE	FARM LABORER	MURDER-BURGLARY	HANGING	NOV 11 1887
LANDRETH, WILLIAM	60	WHITE	MALE	LABORER	MURDER	HANGING	JUL 6 1888
MCGINNIS, PATRICK		WHITE	MALE	JAIL PRISONER	MURDER	HANGING	APR 26 1889
CHEE, GONG		ASIAN	MALE	LABORER	MURDER	HANGING	AUG 9 1889
SULLIVAN, PETER		WHITE	MALE		MURDER	HANGING	NOV 15 1889
GILMAN, JOHN		WHITE	MALE	FARMER	MURDER	HANGING	DEC 13 1889
MING, HOW		ASIAN	MALE	MINER	MURDER	HANGING	JAN 8 1892
ZORN, FRED		WHITE	MALE	FARMER	MURDER	HANGING	AUG 19 1892
REITER, JOHN	21	WHITE	MALE	SEAMAN	MURDER-ROBBERY	HANGING	DEC 1 1893
HANSEN, JOHN	55	WHITE	MALE	FISHERMAN	MURDER-ROBBERY	HANGING	MAY 18 1894
MONTGOMERY, LLOYD	18	WHITE	MALE	FARM WORKER	MURDER	HANGING	JAN 31 1896
PORTER, KELSAY	47	WHITE	MALE	HOMESTEADER	MURDER	HANGING	NOV 20 1897
BRANTON, CLAUDE		WHITE	MALE	RANGE RIDER	MURDER-ROBBERY	HANGING	MAY 12 1899
MAGERS, WILLIAM	26	WHITE	MALE	EX CONVICT	MURDER-ROBBERY	HANGING	FEB 2 1900
GILLESPIE, COLEMAN	20	WHITE	MALE	LABORER	MURDER-ROBBERY	HANGING	JAN 5 1900
DALTON, B., H.	23	WHITE	MALE	?	MURDER-ROBBERY	HANGING	JAN 31 1902
WADE, JOSEPH	20	WHITE	MALE	?	MURDER-	HANGING	JAN 31 1902

Name	Age	Race	Sex	Occupation	Crime	Method	Date
SCHIEVE, AUGUST		WHITE	MALE	?	ROBBERY MURDER	HANGING	JUL 2 1902
BELDING, E., L.	30	WHITE	MALE	BARTENDER	MURDER	HANGING	MAR 27 1903
LYONS, ELLIOTT	35	WHITE	MALE	CARPENTER	MURDER	HANGING	APR 17 1903
SMITH, GEORGE		BLACK	MALE	?	MURDER	HANGING	JUN 5 1903
ARMSTRONG, PLEASANT	28	WHITE	MALE	MINER	MURDER	HANGING	JAN 22 1904
EGBERT, HARRY	27	WHITE	MALE	TEAMSTER	MURDER	HANGING	JAN 29 1904
GUGLIELMO, FRANK	23	WHITE	MALE	SALOON OWNER	MURDER	HANGING	MAY 5 1905
LAUTH, GEORGE	25	WHITE	MALE	GAMBLER	MURDER	HANGING	JUL 13 1905
WILLIAMS, NORMAN	55	WHITE	MALE	FARMER	MURDER	HANGING	JUL 21 1905
BARNES, JOHN		WHITE	MALE	MINER	MURDER-ROBBERY	HANGING	SEP 18 1906
SHEPHERD, FRED	23	WHITE	MALE	RANCH HAND	MURDER	HANGING	NOV 30 1906
HOSE, HENRY	32	WHITE	MALE	VETERAN	MURDER	HANGING	DEC 21 1906
MEGORDEN, HOLLIVER	57	WHITE	MALE	FARMER	MURDER	HANGING	JUN 28 1907
JOHNSON, WALTER	28	WHITE	MALE	CLAIMS LOCATOR	MURDER-ROBBERY	HANGING	FEB 5 1909
TIMMONS, C., Y.	37	WHITE	MALE	PLASTERER	MURDER	HANGING	FEB 26 1909
NORDSTROM, ADOLPH	28	WHITE	MALE	RAILROAD WORKER	MURDER-ROBBERY	HANGING	JUN 18 1909
ANDERSON, JOSEPH	35	WHITE	MALE	EX CONVICT	MURDER-ROBBERY	HANGING	JUL 2 1909
JANCIGAJ, MATTHIAS	28	WHITE	MALE	LABORER	MURDER	HANGING	JAN 22 1909
FINCH, JAMES	39	WHITE	MALE	ATTORNEY	MURDER	HANGING	NOV 12 1909
ROSELAIR, JOHN	47	WHITE	MALE	RANCHER	MURDER	HANGING	SEP 8 1910
HARRELL, ISAAC	48	WHITE	MALE	SHEPHERD	MURDER	HANGING	SEP 9 1910
ROBERTS, H., E.	29	WHITE	MALE	EX CONVICT	MURDER	HANGING	DEC 13 1912
MORGAN, MIKE		WHITE	MALE	ARMY DESERTER	MURDER-ROBBERY	HANGING	DEC 13 1912
GARRISON, FRANK	37	WHITE	MALE	FARMER	MURDER	HANGING	DEC 13 1912
FAULDER, T.J. NOBLE		WHITE	MALE	RAILROAD WORKER	MURDER	HANGING	DEC 13 1912
HUMPHREY, GEORGE	52	WHITE	MALE	FARMER	MURDER-ROBBERY	HANGING	MAR 22 1913
HUMPHREY, CHARLES	39	WHITE	MALE	FARMER	MURDER-ROBBERY	HANGING	MAR 22 1913
SEYMOUR, FRANK	19	HISPANIC	MALE	FIREMAN	MURDER-ROBBERY	HANGING	JAN 31 1913
SPANOS, MIKE	22	WHITE	MALE	TAILOR	MURDER-	HANGING	JAN 31 1913

Name	Age	Race	Sex	Occupation	Crime	Method	Date
HANSEL, OSWALD	55	WHITE	MALE	RANCHER	ROBBERY MURDER	HANGING	NOV 17 1913
BANCROFT, EMMETT	39	WHITE	MALE	FARMER	MURDER	HANGING	NOV 5 1920
RATHIE, JOHN	22	WHITE	MALE	CARPENTER	MURDER	HANGING	JUL 7 1922
KIRBY, ELVIE	23	WHITE	MALE	FARMER	MURDER	HANGING	JUL 7 1922
HOWARD, GEORGE		WHITE	MALE	FARM HAND	MURDER-ROBBERY	HANGING	SEP 8 1922
WALTERS, HUSTED	23	WHITE	MALE	AWOL SOLDIER	MURDER	HANGING	MAR 9 1923
CASEY, DAN		WHITE	MALE	RAILROAD SWITCHM	MURDER-ROBBERY	HANGING	AUG 24 1923
PARKER, GEORGE	32	WHITE	MALE	COOK	MURDER	HANGING	JAN 4 1924
PEARE, L., W.	70	WHITE	MALE	MOONSHINER	MURDER	HANGING	MAY 22 1925
COVELL, ARTHUR		WHITE	MALE	ASTROLOGER	MURDER	HANGING	MAY 22 1925
LLOYD, W., R.	27	WHITE	MALE	EX CONVICT	MURDER-ROBBERY	HANGING	NOV 30 1925
CODY, ARCHIE	44	WHITE	MALE	FARM LABORER	MURDER	HANGING	APR 16 1926
BROWNLEE, ALBERT	27	WHITE	MALE	FIREMAN	MURDER	HANGING	MAY 17 1927
BUTCHEK, JOHN	45	WHITE	MALE	MOLDER	MURDER	HANGING	JUN 10 1927
WILLOS, JAMES	27	WHITE	MALE	SWITCHMAN	MURDER	HANGING	APR 20 1928
KELLEY, ELLSWORTH	29	WHITE	MALE	LABORER	MURDER	HANGING	APR 20 1928
KINGSLEY, JAMES	25	WHITE	MALE	ESCAPED CONVICT	MURDER	HANGING	JAN 30 1931
MCCARTHY, LEROY	26	WHITE	MALE	APP BARBER	MURDER-ROBBERY	ASPHYXIATION-GAS	JUN 20 1939
CLINE, CLAUDE	46	WHITE	MALE	MINER	MURDER-ROBBERY	ASPHYXIATION-GAS	JUL 26 1940
THOMAS, JAMES	19	WHITE	MALE	DESERTED SAILOR	MURDER-ROBBERY	ASPHYXIATION-GAS	JAN 30 1941
SOTO, JOHN	17	HISPANIC	MALE	ESCAPE MENTAL PAT	MURDER-ROBBERY	ASPHYXIATION-GAS	MAR 20 1942
WALLACE, WILLIAM	54	WHITE	MALE	GAMBLER	MURDER	ASPHYXIATION-GAS	FEB 26 1943
CUNNINGHAM, HARVEY	38	BLACK	MALE	SHIPYARD WORKER	MURDER	ASPHYXIATION-GAS	MAR 6 1944
LAYTON, RICHARD	36	WHITE	MALE	POLICEMAN	MURDER-RAPE	ASPHYXIATION-GAS	DEC 8 1944
FOLKES, ROBERT	24	BLACK	MALE	RAILROAD COOK	MURDER-RAPE	ASPHYXIATION-GAS	JAN 5 1945
HIGGINS, WALTER	32	WHITE	MALE	BARBER	MURDER-ROBBERY	ASPHYXIATION-GAS	JAN 15 1945

MERTEN, HENRY	31	WHITE	MALE	MECHANIC	MURDER-ROBBERY	ASPHYXIATION-GAS	JAN 15	1945
DENNIS, ANDREW	45	WHITE	MALE	RAILROAD WORKER	MURDER	ASPHYXIATION-GAS	FEB 2	1946
BAILEY, KENNETH		WHITE	MALE		MURDER	ASPHYXIATION-GAS	SEP 13	1946
HENDERSON, WARDELL	27	BLACK	MALE	ARMY DESERTER	MURDER-ROBBERY	ASPHYXIATION-GAS	JAN 23	1948
LONG, WAYNE	26	WHITE	MALE	PAROLEE	MURDER-ROBBERY	ASPHYXIATION-GAS	AUG 8	1952
PAYNE, FRANK	52	WHITE	MALE	UNEMPLOYED	MURDER-ROBBERY	ASPHYXIATION-GAS	JAN 9	1953
LELAND, MORRIS	22	WHITE	MALE	PAROLEE	MURDER-RAPE	ASPHYXIATION-GAS	JAN 9	1953
KARNES, ALBERT	24	WHITE	MALE	FARM LABORER	MURDER-ROBBERY	ASPHYXIATION-GAS	JAN 30	1953
MCGAUHEY, LEROY	40	WHITE	MALE	LOGGER	MURDER	ASPHYXIATION-GAS	AUG 20	1962
WRIGHT, DOUGLAS	56	NATIVE	MALE	LABORER	MURDER	LETHAL INJ.	SEP 6	1996
MOORE, HARRY C.	56	WHITE	MALE	LABORER	MURDER	LETHAL INJ	MAY 16	1997

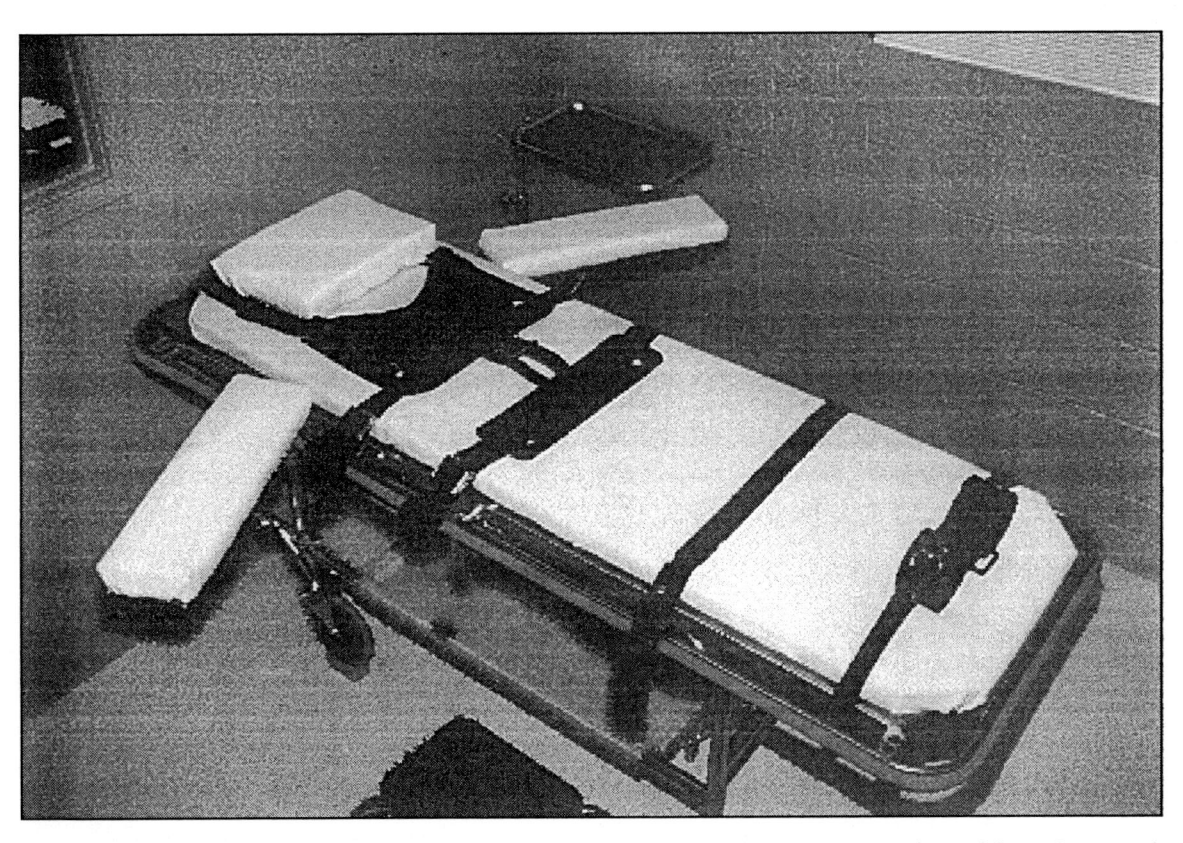

Lethal Injection table used for the execution of Douglas Wright and Harry Moore. The table is designed to slightly elevate the inmate's head so witnesses have full view of the actual execution. Photo: OSP

Uniforms

1912 Photo of Oregon prison guard. Uniforms are dark suits with white shirts and neckties.. Felt hat.

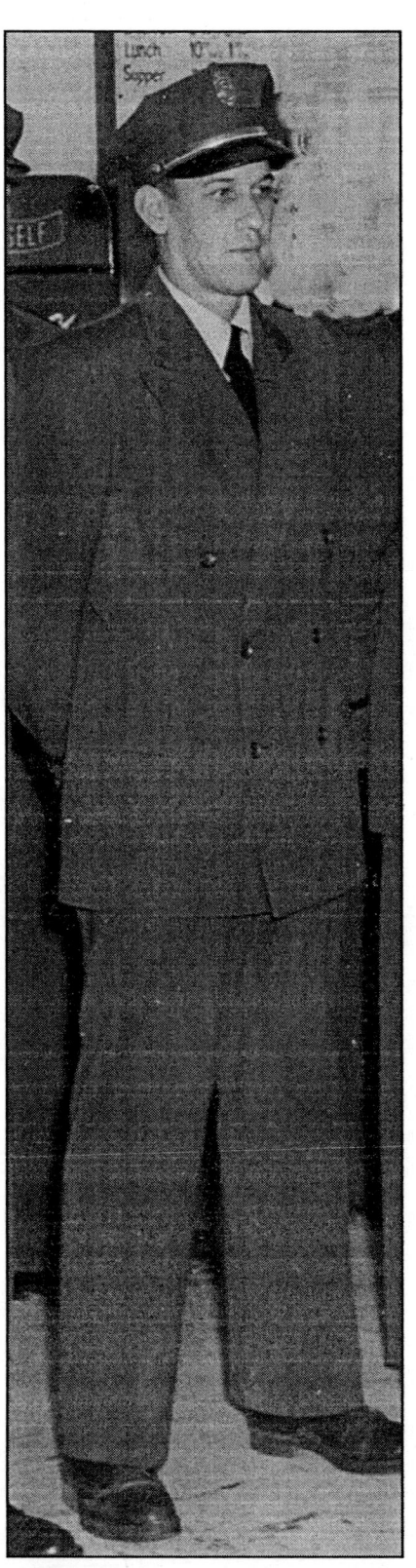

Dave Karn in double breasted dark grey uniform with epaulets on shoulders, light grey shirt and black tie. Military style hat with hat badge. Uniform was made in the prison tailor shop. Circa 1950

Uniforms

Dark brown Eisenhower style jacket, gold cloth patch- with tan slacks with dark brown stripe down the leg. Dark brown neck tie, white shirt, baseball style hat with printed patch. Photo: Tom Burke

Dark brown blazer, brown buttons, gold cloth patch, tan slacks with dark brown stripe down the leg. Dark brown necktie, white shirt, baseball style hat with printed patch. Photo: Tom Burke

Initially the prison had no specific uniforms for guards and wardens, they wore the work clothes of the day. After the Oregon State Police Agency was formed there was a greater interest in guards having uniforms. State police officers trained on the prison grounds and adopted a uniform patterned after the Northwest Mounted Police in Canada. In the 1940's an officer (Kitzman) who worked in the tailor shop had his wife design a uniform patterned after a World War II uniform. That pattern was later adopted for the first guard uniforms made in the OSP tailor shop. The design was later modified and when it no longer was practical to make the uniforms at OSP they were purchased to order from a wholesale uniform company.

Uniforms

Dark brown jacket with zipper, cloth patch, white shirt, dark brown neck tie, baseball style hat with printed patch. Circa 1980s Photo: Tom Burke

Black jacket with zipper, metal badge. Grey shirt with black neck tie, cloth patch on both sleeve with rocker. Baseball style hat with new emblem cloth patch. Circa 1994 to present.
Photo: Tom Burke

Merle "Pete" Weigel in front of OSP front wall in uniform Circa 2003.
Photo: Pete Weigel

OSP 140 th Anniversary Badge, designed by Sergeant Steven Lange 2006

Territorial
Report 125.804

294

(15)

Treasury Department
Comptrollers Office
March 17th 1857

His Excellency
George L. Curry, Governor of
Oregon, and Treasurer of the
Penitentiary fund - Salem

      Sir

I have respectfully to advise you, that an account has been adjusted at the Treasury between the United States and yourself for your disbursement out of the Penitentiary fund embracing a period of time from January 31st to November 20th, 1856 and by which there has been found due the United States a balance of 6,991.61
Amount stated to be due the United States by your account current $1,194.61
Causing a difference of   5,797.25
Which is this explained
Report 122.863 voucher No 34 payment to W.S.Ladd for service as
"President Commissioners" - 8 days $5-$40- and for service as "President Commissioners" 4 months at $100 per year $33.50 total
$73.00 Suspended that the period of service may be stated. May it not be possible that the period of service has been covered by payments made to other parties? It is noticed the order upon to pay refers to "Lexicon, as Acting Commissioner" and to which add the following sums charged in the present adjustment and suspended for want of endorsement of parties to whom the orders are assigned, viz'

Voucher No	52	A.B. Hallack	273.00
"	"53	Joseph Sloan	115.00
"	"54 1/2	S.J. McCormick	90.00
"	"56	Wm Doland	65.00
"	"57	T.J. Dayer	12.00

Note: If corrected vouchers should be filed in these cases, the originals will be returned.

Add warrant for advance No. 7563
dated January 5, 1857 and not yet credited in account Current Note The differences in this behalf is merely nominal and will be relieved when credited in account current.
    $5,168.75
Differences as explained $5,797.25

      Most Sincerely
       Yours

      Elisha Whittelsey
      Comptroller

Transcription of original letter furnished by Richard Egan

[1]In 1956 Lieutenant Hoyt Cupp served as Editor of the OSP staff newspaper titled "Gladiator". June 15 and July 13 of that year he published a two part article on what the prison looked like when he was first employed in 1948. These articles provide a unique opportunity for us to view the prison through Cupps eyes sixty years later.

The Prison Eight Years Ago

Editor's Note: I have just celebrated my eighth year of employment at the prison. What did it look like when I was first employed? What was the policy at that time? This is the first of two articles on the prison during the year 1948. The first article will deal entirely with the physical plant.

A vast rebuilding of the prison has been accomplished the past eight years. As the physical plant of the institution has changed so has the policy. Let us take a tour through the prison during the year 1948 and see if we can visualize the changes which have transpired:

Part One

The wall is 12 feet high made of brick with barbed wire running across the top and there are eight towers on the wall. These towers are about three times the size of the future towers. Number two tower has a wood stove plus steam heat radiation and the gate is cranked by hand.

As we walk into the Administration Building, the Warden's (Superintendent's) Office is on the right, the curio shop is in the lobby and the arsenal is located directly across from the main gate. The arsenal officer controls the gate going into the prison. As we enter the prison we walk along a passageway which connects the administration building with the intermediate building - the post office, trusty quarters, visitors waiting room and the turnkey's office.

The first room we come to is the mail room, operated by Eddy Hayes and two inmates.

We continue along and come to the turnkey's office. This office is about as large as the lobby of the administration building; the turnkey's duties are to receive all outside phone calls, deliver in all the new commitments, handle all visits and keep an eye on the Chapel. From the turnkey's office we go through a sally port into the Chapel. The Chapel is the hub of the operation; all cell blocks lead into this room; and all visits are held here. The Chapel is a room about the size of the future control room. From the Chapel an officer can look down either side of "A" or "B" blocks. To enter the new block, which is "C", you must walk through "B" block and then across a passageway. As we walk around we notice a big new cell block which is just about to be completed and is to be called "D" block. We walk down the back stairs of the Chapel and we are out in the yard area. The first person that we see is Captain Sundborg directing a group of inmates at the sawdust bin. It seems that all new inmates are assigned to this job for the first few weeks. As we continue along we see the laundry, shower room, shoe shop and yard captain's office in the building just across the road from the new commissary building; the second floor of this building includes the clothing room and tailor shop. Mr. T.V. Ryan and officer Morton are the supervisors over the clothing room, commissary, kitchen, shoe and tailor shops.

We walk between the boiler room and the Yard Captain's office out to the island. At the gate heading across the bridge we see Officer Folquet on duty. The yard consists of one concrete slab and we notice a large group of inmates pacing back and forth. This is the extent of the recreation area. Just to the left of the flume, we notice officer Kenyon on duty. We leave the yard area and walk back past the boiler room, turn right toward the flax mill and pass the big fish pond in front of "C" block.

Our first stop is at the machine shop, which is located just to the south of the flax mill. As we enter, we see Fred Phillips supervising a group of inmates working on a piece of farm equipment. The shop is very dark and just about one half of it has a cement floor. At the far end of the shop one of the blacksmiths is making a hitch for one of the horse drawn wagons at the farm. As we leave the machine shop we turn left on the road leading over to two gate. The gate is located just about 20 feet from the end of "B" block. Here we notice officer Francis on duty. He is busy punching a load of flax going out the gate. The inmate drivers assigned to this gate stay in a room in the basement of "B" block. Number two gate has a cage on the inside of the wall. the outside gate is made of a large piece of plate steel with a railroad iron across the middle.

Leaving number two gate, we walk back towards the flax mill. Just in front of the mill we see the baseball diamond. Number three tower is right in back of home plate. A ball hitting on the flax mill roof is good for a home run. Outside the mill we observe Eddie Mays, George Bixler and Pete Luthie supervising the inmates during one of the smoking periods. Walking past the mill about 30 yards we come to the north wall. The wall is painted with white wash and gleams in the sun. We see a number of inmates at work on the lawn, mowing, raking and watering. We leave the institution by the only wall gate, which is number two gate, and the first thing we notice on the outside of the wall is the old dormitory and the cannery. We take a right turn around the wall and head toward the flax sheds, just to the left are the horse barn and the root houses. We complete our tour and head back toward the administration building.

As we leave we cannot know of the tremendous physical improvements which will occur in the next few years.

The policy, too was to change drastically. Next month we'll discuss these changes by comparing the past with the present.

Part 2

This second and last of two articles, deals with the policy of the prison during the year 1948. Let us return to this era and try to visualize the operation of the institution during this period.

The policy of the institution in 1948 was one basically of a punitive nature. Special privileges were granted to a few inmates, and informers were also cultivated in this manner. Discipline was not standardized, and often fluctuated with the whims of those in authority. Supervision of the inmates was at a minimum, and the individualized treatment program did not exist.

The lack of sufficient supervision caused many problems throughout the institution during this period. To cite one example, only one employee supervised five different working areas. It therefore was necessary to delegate authority to the inmates in each area. This inevitably let to the "con bosses," and all the evils which always attend this system.

The inmates fortunate enough to attain these chosen jobs were often granted special privileges. They were often allowed to sleep in their work area, rather than in their cells. They were allowed to eat on the "short line." where the food was better than the main line. This second meal was intended for those assigned to heavy tasks such as Outside Gangs, Construction Crews, etc.

Inmate informers were used on all departmental levels. Each employee relied on one or more for his own source of information. This improper use of this practice caused much unrest and hard feelings among the inmates and often led to actual bloodshed. This too often placed the inmate in the position of expecting privileges as his right.

While the lack of supervision created a major problem within the institution, a form of discipline was maintained by using such methods as the silent system in the dining room and forcing the inmates to walk in line with arms folded. Special work assignments were arranged for the less manageable. Breaches of discipline were punished by a session in the "Bull Pen" (Segregation Unit). While corporal punishment was not administered by the institution as such, it often was by individual officers. Sentences ranged from one day to as long as three years and only two meals a day were fed.

The disciplinary problem was a major one. This was in large part due to the lack of recreational facilities. The recreation program during this period consisted of "Yannigan" baseball, and one show weekly. The largest number of inmates spent their yard time walking aimlessly back and forth on the island, which was the old yard.

The lack of proper recreational program was by no means the only problem confronting the officials. The library consisted of less than one thousand books. Most of these had been donated by other organizations or public-minded citizens, with no particular emphasis on censorship. The classification department and its related facilities did not exist. The school and hobby shop were in the future. The classification of inmates was handled by the yard Captain and Deputy Warden, who also managed the job assignments for outside workers, and most inside assignments.

Other problems too numerous to mention were met by officials during this year. The lack of trained personnel, and the lack of physical facilities also created a problem. In many ways, the major problems have not changed, as custody and care of the prisoners is still foremost in our minds in all prison administration

Yes there have been many changes in the institution in the past eight years. The policy of our institution today is one of fair, impersonal and impartial treatment. Close supervision is our keynote of success. The employees of the institution today may look back and evaluate past against present policy and wonder what the future has in store.

Recreation Yard OSP
Photo: Grant Yoder

A Tribute to Sergeant Joe Johnson

Sergeant Joe Johnson was a correctional officer at the prison in the 1950s and early 1960s. While at OSP, Joe met and married his wife who was initially employed in the Women's ward section of the prison and also served as Superintendent O'Malley's secretary. Johnson researched the history of the Oregon State Penitentiary and wrote about it. Joe Johnson left OSP in 1963 to work at Folsom Prison in California. In an article that appeared in *The Gladiator,* Volume 4 Number 4, April 16, 1958 is a description of some of Johnson's writings.

OSP History Told in Law Enforcement Magazine

"From the log jail house in 1846 that stood in Oregon City to the group of massive concrete and steel buildings that stand in Salem in 1958 is the scope of a comprehensive history of the Oregon State Penitentiary appearing in the current issue of the Pacific Coast Law Enforcement News Magazine. The article by Sgt. J. R. Johnson is an extremely informing and interesting story that is a must reading for all present day employees of the institution."

"The bulk of the story is a reprint of another story that appeared in the Historical Quarterly and is the result of a report which Sgt. Johnson prepared for Warden Gladden in 1955. The article is excellently illustrated with a series of photographs showing the structural improvement of the penitentiary through a span of 113 years. Also shown are several revealing air pictures of the prison as it appears today. Reprints of the article will be secured and made available to employees through the Training Command in the immediate future."

One of the articles written by Sergeant Joe R. Johnson provides an interesting insight into Major Montgomery P. Berry's challenges as Superintendent. It was printed in the *The Gladiator*, Volume 1 Number 3, November 3, 1955

"You Are There OSP 88 Years Ago 1867

" The man astride the mount held his reins in one hand and his hat with the other and he leaned forward in the saddle with his head bowed to protect his face from the fury of the windswept rain that cascaded down from the sullen sky. He kept the bay horse at a gallop as he splashed heedlessly through the sprawling puddles of East State Street in Salem. Under his breath he muttered words to the effect that it was damn unnecessary to locate the prison so far from town."

"When he finally brought the panting steed to a halt in front of a drab little building identified by a weathered inscription, Superintendent's Office - Oregon State Penitentiary, he dismounted and tethered the animal to a post and hurriedly entered the building. Once inside, he doffed his drenched hat with an appropriate comment about the weather and addressed the stern, austere looking gentleman behind the desk. "Mr. Berry, I'm afraid I have bad news for you."

"The man behind the desk was Superintendent Major M. P. Berry and the calendar on the wall behind him showed the date to be Wednesday, January 10, 1867. He looked up at the lieutenant for a petulant, instant and then back to the menu he was preparing. "Well, Lieutenant?" His tone was crisp, nearly acid.

"Farmer Smith said that he can not spare beef at this time, sir." The officer spoke regretfully as though it was something personal."

"I tried to bargain with several other farmers in the vicinity and as far north as Gervais, but they are all reluctant to part with their meat at this time of the year." Minutes of silence ensued, interrupted only by the rain beating on the roof and the annoying rattle of something clattering against the building outside.

"I guess this will have to suffice," he said, more to himself than for the benefit of the lieutenant who still stood patiently waiting for further orders. He proceeded to read aloud. "6:30 A.M. breakfast: bacon, beans, coffee and bread. Weekday dinners: coffee, bread, and potatoes" After potatoes he had written fresh beef. He scratched it out. "Sunday dinner: rice, syrup, and coffee." He placed the menu on the desk and removed his glasses as he stood up and strode slowly across the room to the stained glass window that overlooked the prison yard. The lieutenant was beside him. "It's a mess alright, sir. I don't blame you for being disgusted." They stood surveying the barn-like building that housed the prisoners and the dilapidated fence that stretched as far as the gully and ended.

"I guess I should be philosophical about these problems that continually confront me, Lieutenant, but sometimes it seems like a hopeless cause. Providing adequate food to sustain the prisoners is one thing and security is another. That fence is a laughing stock. I've appealed to Governor Wood again and again for funds to complete it."

"The legislators will be meeting again next week sir. Wouldn't the Governor permit you to speak to them yourself and explain the urgency of funds to improve the security of the institution?"

"Lieutenant," his voice seemed to have lost its metallic incisiveness and instead took on the soft quality of a seer prophesying the future. "Some day the State of Oregon may have to deal with not fifty or sixty prisoners, but maybe five hundred or even a thousand. I wonder what security they will have developed then. Maybe in 1950 or 1960 the administration will look back and laugh at my problems and our prison of wood buildings and a fourteen foot high fence."

OSP history contains a few references to Sergeant Joe Johnson after he moved to California and accepted a position at Folsom prison. When staff visited Folsom, Joe always inquired about friends back in Salem and those well wishes were printed in the staff newsletter *The Gladiator*.

OSP Isolation and Segregation Unit in 1967 housed more inmates then the entire prison held in 1867
Photo: Sergeant J.R.Johnson

Entrance to the Oregon Prison Farm Annex. The brick work was done by Wayne Montwheeler an inmate at the farm and a skilled brick layer artisan. During this period the farm was a showplace They won awards for the dairy herds, beef cattle, swine, poultry section and truck farm goods. Produce, meat, poultry, milk, eggs and bacon was supplied to the various state institutions. The fence lines were straight, the buildings were painted and well maintained.. The Annex was originally known as the State Training School for Boys

State Training School for Boys Cemetery is marked only by this dilapidated gate into a graveyard containing four tombstones of those known as Oregon's forgotten children.

Bennie Jackson 1891-1908

Hiram McRae 1891-1908

Oregon's Forgotten Children

Frank Dilley 1892-1910

James O'Brien 1892-1908

These young boys died of Tuberculosis, Diphtheria, Hemorrhage. Their death certificates list no parents of record. They came from Alaska, Medford, and St. Paul,

Cemetery inside the Oregon State Prison reservation
When the prison was first established in Salem a graveyard was located outside the walls near a grove of trees. That area later was included inside the walls and a baseball diamond built over the area. The grave of Harry Tracy was located near third base on the field. No markers were placed in the cemetery.

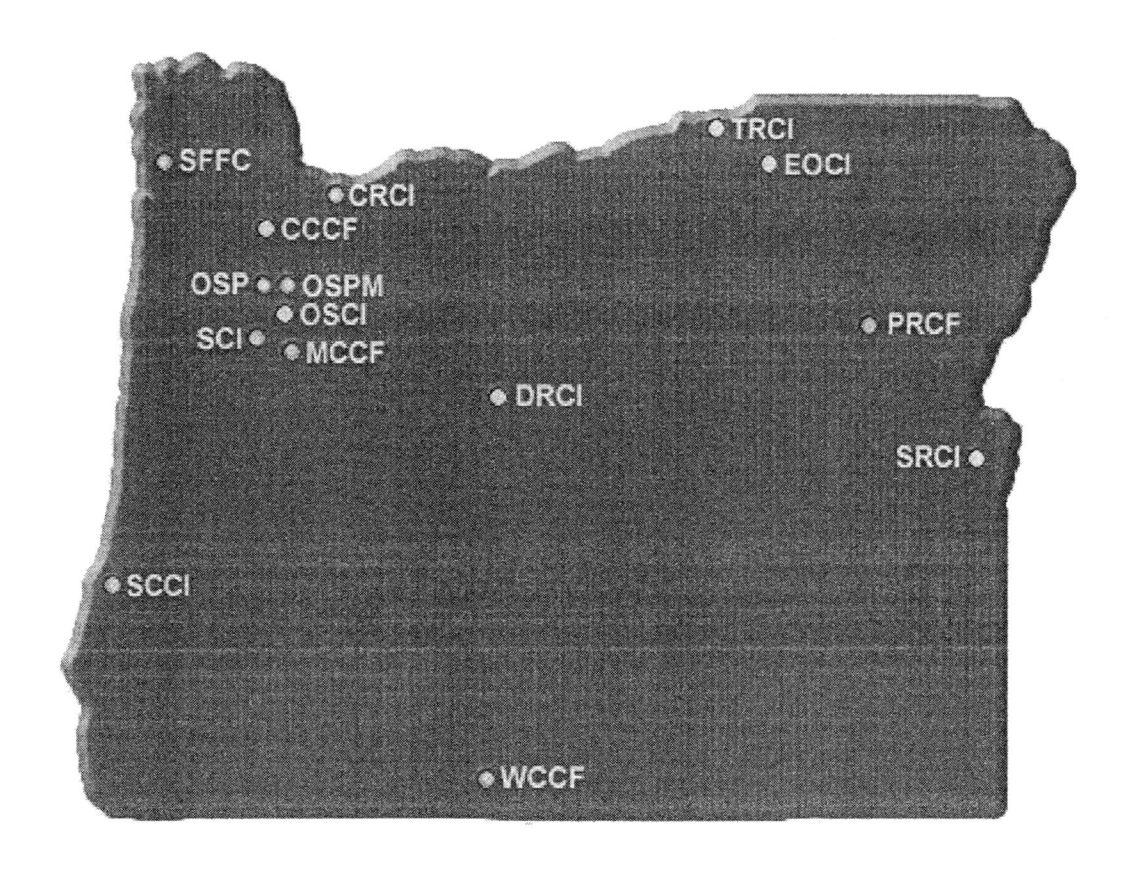

Oregon needed one prison in 1866, by 2009 the needs had grown to 14

1866   OSP opens in Salem
1928   MCCF (State Boys Training School, later Prison Farm Annex) turned over to OSP
1949   SFFC established
1859   OSCI built and opened in Salem
1964   OWCC built next door to OSP
1977   SCI (Prigg Cottage, later CDRC, DCRC) retrofitted and turned over to DOC
1977   WRU opens at state hospital (closed in 1991)
1985   EOCI retrofitted and turned over to DOC
1989   PRCF built and opened in Baker City
1990   SCCF retrofitted and opened in North Bend
1990   CRCI built and opened in Portland
1991   SRCI built and opened in Ontario
2000   TRCI built and opened in Hermiston
2001   CCCF built and opened in Wilsonville
2002   OSPM converted from OWCC
2005   WCCF built and opened in Lakeview
2007   DRCF built and opened in Madras

OSP Superintendents have a history of encouraging and supporting a variety of inmate recreational programs. One of the programs is the inmate art program. Examples of inmate work are shown.

Oil painting by Vincent Capitan

Oregon state seal above etched in marble from the first capitol building, Ivory work below by Michael Umscheid - scrimshaw artist

Leather tooling by Jerry Oliver

Color pencil sketch by S. Nagel

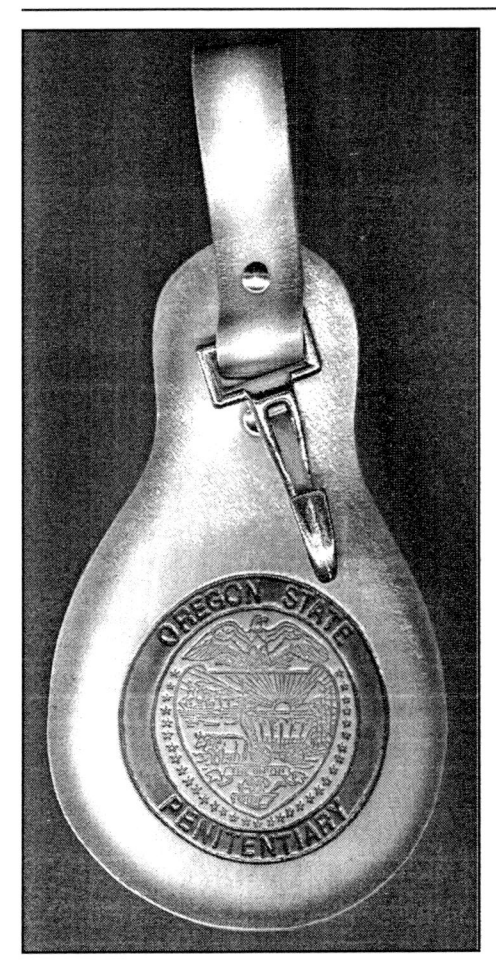

Officers beaver tail leather key holder with Oregon seal by J. Brudos (photo reduced)

Inmate art work made from sculpted styro foam cups artist unknown

Badge case of tooled leather by D. Little

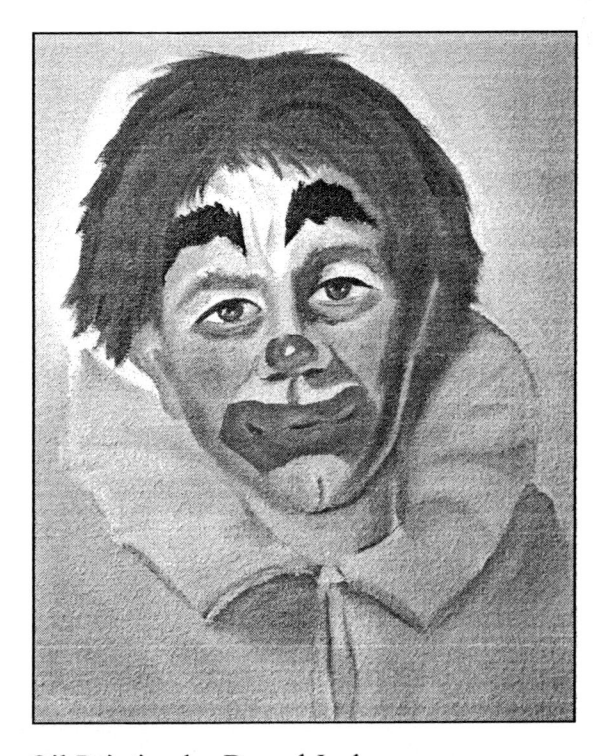

Oil Painting by Drexel Jackson